On Monday, October 26, 1987, Dr. Norman Vincent Peale, author of *The Power of Positive Thinking* and founder and publisher of *Guideposts* magazine, presented the 1987 *Guideposts* Church Award to Pastor Dale Galloway and New Hope Community Church in Portland, Oregon.

"Every human being has a hurt," Dr. Peale said. "An institution that is dedicated to healing the hurts is deserving of the highest award that can be given."

New Hope Community Church was also recognized in 1986 as the fastest growing church in the state of Oregon by the Reverend Jerry Falwell, pastor of Thomas Road Baptist Church in Lynchburg, Virginia, the second largest church in America, and by Elmer Towns of the Christian Leadership Institute in Lynchburg, who has compiled a listing of the fastest growing churches for several years.

From a drive-in church with little or no congregation or financial support to the fastest growing church in Oregon in little over a decade. How did they do it? What is their secret? How can their success help you personally or your church collectively?

Read *Broken Members, Mended Body* and find out. Catch the vision! Dare to dream! Give God your brokenness and let Him turn it into blessing.

BROKEN MEMBERS
MENDED BODY

FOREWORD BY JACK W. HAYFORD

BROKEN MEMBERS MENDED BODY

BUILDING A MINISTRY
WITH LOVE AND RESTORATION

KATHI MILLS

GL
Regal Books
A Division of GL Publications
Ventura, California, U.S.A.

Published by Regal Books
A Division of GL Publications
Ventura, California 93006
Printed in U.S.A.

Although real names have been used in some instances, in other instances, names have been changed to protect confidentiality. Composite characters have also been created, although they are representatives of real people attending New Hope Community Church.

Library of Congress Cataloging-in-Publication Data

Mills, Kathi, 1948-
    Broken Members, Mended Body : Building a ministry with love and restoration / Kathi Mills.
    p.   cm.
    Includes bibliographies.
    ISBN 0-8307-1302-6
    1. Pastoral theology.   I. Title.
BV4011.M52   1989
253—dc19   89-3530
                                                              CIP

1 2 3 4 5 6 7 8 9 10 / 91 90 89

Rights for publishing this book in other languages are contracted by Gospel Literature International (GLINT) foundation. GLINT also provides technical help for the adaptation, translation, and publishing of Bible study resources and books in scores of languages worldwide. For further information, contact GLINT, Post Office Box 488, Rosemead, California, 91770, U.S.A., or the publisher.

To my father,
Hans Gramckow

With love and thanks
for all you've been in my life

A special thanks to all the warm and wonderful people at New Hope Community Church who so graciously gave of their time to help in the research and writing of this book. You welcomed me and made me feel at home—as you do everyone who walks through your doors.

CONTENTS

And He Himself gave some to be apostles, some prophets, some
evangelists, and some pastors and teachers, for the equipping of
the saints for the work of ministry, for the edifying of
the body of Christ.
Ephesians 4:11,12

He took bread, blessed and broke it, and gave it to them. Then
their eyes were opened and they knew Him.
Luke 24:30,31

FOREWORD

Throughout the many years that I have been in the ministry, I have been confronted with virtually every conceivable human problem. I have long since ceased to be shocked by the confessions and revelations of those—whether Christian or nonChristian—who have come to me to pour out their broken hearts, to bare their bleeding souls, and to unload their burdens of guilt and sin. But I pray I will never allow the frequency with which I encounter these broken, bleeding people to callous me to the depth and the severity of their pain.

If there is one thing I've learned in all those years of ministry and counseling, it is that there is a world full of hurting people out there, people at the precipice of destruction, desperately searching, hoping for someone to come along and offer them hope and a reason to go on.

Although each circumstance is as different as each individual person, they all have one thing in common: the need for love and restoration.

Jesus recognized that need in people. Whether He was teaching among crowds, passing along the seashore, or walking the dusty streets of Jerusalem, He was responsive to human hurt. He seemed to hear people's deepest pains and to sense their most profound needs. It was as if their silent despair called to Him from the midst of the throngs even when their lips were sealed. But whether spoken or unspoken, He always heard them, and always He answered. His ever-gentle even-handedness mastered the most delicate situations and met the most demanding needs.

Take, for example, that morning when Jesus sat teaching, and the religious leaders brought to Him a woman who had been caught in the act of adultery. They reminded Him that Moses' law required that she be stoned. They waited.

Jesus appeared not to hear. He bent down. With His finger, He wrote something in the sand. Then, standing, He said to them, "He who is without sin among you, let him throw a stone at her first."[1] Moments later, the crowd had melted, the critics disappeared, and the accused woman was standing there alone with Jesus and His disciples. "Where are your accusers?" He asked. "Has no one condemned you?"[2] "No one, Lord," was her answer.

What Jesus said next is a master stroke: "Neither do I condemn you; go and sin no more."[3]

Jesus did not ignore her sin. Neither condemning nor condoning it. He majestically balanced judgment and mercy. Then He offered words of healing and new life. "Go," He said, "and sin no more." I forgive you. Start over. Start fresh. Put the past behind you and begin again. That was exactly what that woman needed to hear to set her free from the bondage of her life of sin. Jesus knew that, and He met her at the point of her need.

Jesus showed the same understanding for "people where they are" in Thomas's case. When the other disciples told Thomas that Jesus was alive, his response was, "Unless I see in His hands the print of the nails, and put my finger into the print of the nails, and put my hand into His side, I will not believe."[4] So Jesus said to him, "Reach your finger here, and look at My hands; and reach your hand here, and put it into My side. Do not be unbelieving, but believing."[5]

The prophet Isaiah predicted Messiah as "a man of sorrows and acquainted with grief."[6] It is because Jesus so completely fulfills the prophecies as God-became-Man that He is able to identify with each of us at the point of our need. He has already walked in our sandals, experienced our sorrows, tasted our grief. Today, this same Jesus, the Son of God, is the one *true* source of unselfish, unconditional, agape love. He is ready to come to any of us—to *each* of us—at that point of our need, saying, "I love you. I forgive you. Now follow me."

And that is the message of *Broken Members, Mended Body*. It is a message of hurts being healed, of dreams being built, and lives being reborn. It is a message of love and forgiveness and restoration. And that, loved ones, is the ministry to which God has called all believers—not just ordained clergy, but anyone and everyone who has experienced the love and forgiveness of God and been reconciled to Him through the shed blood of His only Son, Jesus Christ.

Second Corinthians 5:18 tells us that God "has reconciled us to Himself through Jesus Christ, and has given us the ministry of reconciliation." If God has indeed entrusted us with that ministry, then it is up to us as children of the

King to learn how best to carry out that ministry. This book not only describes the author's study of how New Hope Community Church in Portland, Oregon, has sought to successfully implement such ministry; it also explains how Christians in churches of all denominations and sizes can become active and effective in that ministry, as well.

Broken Members, Mended Body, however, is more than a how-to book on effective lay ministry. Kathi Mills, with her exceptional talent and ability to paint pictures with words, has distilled the heart and soul of the congregational vision at New Hope Community Church, breathing life into the pages of this book with her heart-warming, yet heart-rending, portrayals of the once bruised and battered people who have come to New Hope seeking love and restoration—and found it. They, in turn, are now ministering that same love and restoration to others. They are answering God's call to the ministry of reconciliation. They are obeying the command that Jesus gave to Peter in John 21:17, "Feed my sheep."

Read this book, and then ask yourself: As a loved and forgiven child of the King, can I do any less?

Jack W. Hayford
Senior Pastor of the Church on the Way
Van Nuys, California

NOTES
1. John 8:7.
2. John 8:10.
3. John 8:11.
4. John 20:25.
5. John 20:27.
6. Isaiah 53:3.

INTRODUCTION

"Is this your first time here?" he asked.

My heart ached as I looked at the white-haired gentleman sitting next to me. His lined skin and work-worn hands told of a life of outdoor labor. His pale blue eyes were rimmed with red. Lack of sleep? Worry? Tears? And yet, in spite of his hunched shoulders and tortured, defeated appearance, I knew somehow that he wasn't nearly as old as he seemed.

"Yes—no. Well, not exactly," I answered, wondering just how much to tell him, yet feeling the need to explain my presence. Was he really interested, or did he just need someone to talk to? "Actually, I'm here to learn about this church so I can write a book about it. I—"

"A book?" A brief smile crossed his lips, and I was sure

I caught a faint flicker of interest in his sad, tired eyes. Or was it a fleeting, bittersweet memory darting across the worn, yellowed pages of his mind—a memory of lost but happier times?

"Martha loved books," he said softly. "Everywhere we went, she always had a book with her." He smiled again, and this time I knew he was reliving some oft-remembered occasion with Martha.

Must have been his wife, I thought. *Probably a recent widower. How sad!* I wondered what words of comfort to offer, but before I could speak, he went on.

"We went everywhere together, you know, just the two of us." For a moment, tears glistened at the corners of his red-rimmed eyes, but he ignored them and continued. "Never had any children. Martha was my whole life . . . ."

His voice trailed off, his eyes held a vacant stare; he had forgotten me. I struggled to hold back my own tears as I glanced around the huge auditorium. When I'd walked in 15 minutes earlier, there had been only a handful of people present. I had wondered then if the 300 or more empty chairs weren't a bit optimistic. After all, most churches couldn't fill their sanctuaries with 300 people for a Sunday morning service. Did New Hope Community Church really expect that many to show up on a Monday night?

Now I saw there wasn't an empty seat left. In fact, more seats were being set up in the back of the room to handle the overflow crowd.

And still they kept coming. A big, burly man in a black leather vest with tattoos on his arms. A balding, middle-aged man in a tattered blue suit. A grossly obese woman, barely able to sit on the metal folding chair. An older, poorly dressed couple, clinging tightly to each other. A tall, scrawny man in his 20s with long, unkempt hair, reeking of alcohol and sweat. A young, grim-faced woman with bruises on her neck and arms and the telltale shadow of a recent black eye.

New Life Victorious. That's what they called that Monday night gathering of mismatched, hurting, desperate souls. And that's what they were there for. A chance at a new, victorious life. A chance to find hope and healing for their bruised, battered bodies, emotions and memories.

I had only been at New Hope for a few days before that Monday night meeting. I would be there for several more. Never once during that time did I find the church empty or the doors closed. Never once did I see a person come in with a need that couldn't be met through one of the many outreach ministries available at New Hope. Never once did I see anyone turned away, rejected, condemned or "preached at."

Dale Galloway, senior pastor of Portland, Oregon's New Hope Community Church, believes that "Our greatest need is to be loved and give love."[1] Challenged by their pastor, New Hope's nearly 5,000 members are answering that challenge, reaching out to the lost, the hurting, the disillusioned, beaten-down masses of their community. The community is responding. Of the hundreds of new members joining New Hope's ranks each year, 80 percent of them are previously unchurched. Why are they coming? Because they have needs, and they know that at New Hope those needs will be met. "If you are meeting needs," says Pastor Galloway, "you will never have a shortage of people." Watching the auditorium continue to fill up, I suspected he was right.

I glanced once again at the white-haired gentleman beside me, wondering just how long it had been since his wife had died. Should I ask? Or should I respect his privacy and leave him alone in his grief?

If you are meeting needs, you will never have a shortage of people.

"Divorce is a terrible thing," the man said suddenly, his voice husky with emotion. "It's a disease, a horrible, horrible disease. And it's spreading like wildfire, you know."

I nodded my head, wondering what had brought on this sudden outburst. Had he recognized someone nearby who was recently divorced? Had he been thinking of someone dear to him suffering through that very trauma?

"I never thought Martha would leave me," he said, choking back a sob as tears threatened him once again. He shook his head sadly. "After 32 years, who would ever have thought? . . . "

His voice trailed off again, as I began to absorb the shock of what he had just told me. Divorce! Martha hadn't died. She'd left him! After 32 years, she had simply walked out and divorced him. No wonder his eyes were red, his shoulders slumped. No wonder his face, his entire demeanor, seemed so dejected, so utterly devoid of hope.

But then, I reminded myself, that's why all these people are here. The world is full of lost and hurting people, people whose hopes and dreams have been shattered by the hard realities of life. Many of them were going down for the last time when New Hope tossed them a lifeline. Gratefully, they had latched on to that lifeline and were holding on for all they were worth.

And just how much are they worth? I looked around the room once again. By society's standards, most of them weren't worth much. But as far as Dale Galloway and the congregation of New Hope Community Church are concerned, they are worth everything. They are worth so much that God sent His only Son to die for each and every one of them in order that they might have new life. The members of New Hope are bound and determined to see that those lost and hurting people get every chance to receive that new life.

The meeting was about to begin. A young man with a guitar strummed a few chords as the words to a contemporary praise song were projected onto a screen at the front of the auditorium. The room suddenly felt charged with electricity as all eyes turned forward. The old man next to me no longer struggled with tears. Instead, as his voice lifted in song, becoming stronger and more vibrant with each word, I sensed an air of expectancy about him. It was contagious.

O sing unto the Lord a new song;
for he hath done marvellous things . . .

I joined in the singing of the familiar words from Psalm 98 (*KJV*). By the time the brief worship service, consisting of singing, praise and impromptu testimonies, had ended and people had begun to break up into their smaller, need-meeting groups—groups for recovering alcoholics, substance abusers, overeaters, Vietnam vets—I'd forgotten about research and writing and all my reasons for being there that night. I felt very much a part of the people in that room. But there was something more . . . .

That's when I remembered the words to another Psalm: "The Lord is near to those who have a broken heart" (34:18). And I knew what I had been sensing.

Jesus was in that room, touching, healing, offering love and hope and eternal life to any who would reach out and take it. He was that close. The answer was that simple. And those broken-hearted people understood that. That's why they had come.

The old man turned and looked at me once again. I was surprised to notice that he appeared younger than he had a few moments earlier. Although there was no sign of recognition in his tired blue eyes, a spark of hope now burned brightly behind the pain. As a warm smile spread across his face, he asked once again, "Is this your first time here?"

I returned his smile. "Yes," I answered, no longer feeling the need to explain. "Yes, it is. But it won't be my last."

NOTE

1. Dale E. Galloway, *20/20 VISION How to Create a Successful Church* (Portland, Oregon: Scott Publishing Co., 1986), 117.

CHAPTER ONE

THE BIRTH OF A DREAM

Where there is no vision, the people perish.
Proverbs 29:18, *KJV*

On October 14, 1972, New Hope Community Church held its first service. Pastors Dale and Margi Galloway had no money. They had no congregation. But they had a dream. That dream is still alive—and growing.

Many people told them it couldn't be done. You can't possibly start a church without financial backing, without a congregation, they said. And to attempt to start that church in an outdoor drive-in theater in rainy Portland, Oregon, one of the most unchurched cities in America, was sheer foolishness!

But start it they did. Standing firm on the belief that their dream was of God, Dale preached, Margi sang, the people came, and God blessed. Today, the sanctuary of New Hope Community Church seats 3,000 people. As well as continuous activities throughout the week, services are held twice on Sunday mornings to accommodate

all the worshipers. Parking lots have been added and
enlarged. An additional 28 acres adjacent to the present 14
already owned by New Hope have been purchased for
future expansion. The drawing board is never empty of
plans.

A dream. A vision. That's where it all began. Pastor
Galloway describes a vision as the "ability, or the God-
given gift, to see those things which are not as becoming a
reality."[1] Hebrews 11:1 says it this way: "Now faith is the
substance of things hoped for, the evidence of things not
seen." How did Dale and Margi catch that vision? What
brought them to that place in their faith where they could
believe in and act on their God-given dream, even in the
face of criticism and derision?

The Promise of Blessing

On Christmas Sunday, 1970, less than two years before
Dale Galloway preached his first sermon at New Hope's
drive-in church, he stood before the congregation he then
pastored, a broken man. As he proclaimed the joys of
Christmas, inside he was bleeding. It was the saddest day
of his life.

A stranger had walked up to him on the Friday just
before Christmas and handed him divorce papers. Within
24 hours after receiving those papers, he stood at the
Portland International Airport, crying, as he watched his
wife of 13 years, along with their two children, board a
plane for a one-way flight out of his life.

It was at that very moment, at a point in time when,
for Dale Galloway, death seemed preferable to life, that
the dream was born. It was born because, in spite of the
pain, in spite of the agony, Dale knew he had to go on. He
chose life over death. It was the more difficult choice, but

from that choice, rising up from the ashes of his brokenness, came the promise of blessing.

Weeds of Adversity

But even as the dream took root and began to grow, the weeds of adversity were growing also, trying to choke out the dream. Within a few months of losing his family, Dale was told by a longtime friend and high official in his denomination that, due to the divorce, he should give up any ideas of a future pastoral ministry. Although the friend offered to help him find a teaching job in one of the denomination's colleges, Dale felt as if he'd received a death sentence—the second in a period of months.

From the age of 15, Dale had felt God's call to pastoral ministry. Fulfilling that call had been the central focus of his life ever since. Now he was being told that it, too, was over.

Dale Galloway was 31 years old. His life had seemed filled with good things and promises of even better things to come. He had pastored two successful pastorates and then gone on to lead one of his denomination's larger churches in the state of Oregon. He had a wife, an 8-year-old son and a 5-year-old daughter, all of whom he loved dearly—the perfect family. Then, suddenly, he had lost it all.

After ranting and raving and turning his anger on God, Dale finally came to a point of realizing that he couldn't go on without God's help. He asked God to forgive him for his failures, for his rebellion against Him. Then he placed his life, once more, in God's hands. At that moment, he heard God say to him, "Lo, I am with you always, even to the end of the world" (see Matt. 28:20).

The dream would survive.

With nothing but Dale's ability to preach to people's needs, Margi's ability to sing and a dream they believed had been given them by God, New Hope Community Church held its first service on that October morning in 1972.

Sharing the Dream

God brought loving friends and counselors into Dale's life during the next months. Then, one day, God brought a very special lady into his life, a lady who would become not only his dearest friend, but, eventually, his beloved wife.

Margi was a sixth-grade teacher, the daughter of a pastor. She knew the trials and difficulties of being a pastor's child and, at an early age, had promised herself she would never be a pastor's wife. God had other plans.

Having recently lost her mother, Margi knew about brokenness. She missed the close relationship she had shared with her mother, and longed for Christian companionship. As the friendship between Margi and Dale grew, they discovered their mutual desire to serve God. Soon, the bond of friendship turned to love, and, on August 14, 1971, they were married. Dale's dream became Dale and Margi's dream.

The Dream Grows

As a direct result of the brokenness that Dale had come through, the dream came into sharp focus. He felt God was calling him to "pioneer a healing fellowship for the 'unchurched thousands' where the broken could come and be healed, where the discouraged could come and be lifted, where those searching for love could come and receive Christ's love."[2] And so, with nothing but Dale's ability to preach to people's needs, Margi's ability to sing and a dream they believed had been given them by God, New Hope Community Church held its first service on that October morning in 1972.

Dale's vision for New Hope was to have 1,000 members at the end of 10 years. At the end of nine and one-half years, they reached that goal. That's when Dale realized he had been limiting their growth by setting a ceiling on his dream. He lifted that ceiling, and it took less than two years to bring in the second 1,000 members. The third 1,000 members came even more quickly. And they continue to come. As the dream grows, so does the church.

NOTES

1. Dale E. Galloway, *20/20 VISION How to Create a Successful Church* (Portland, Oregon: Scott Publishing Co., 1986), 29.
2. Dale E. Galloway, *REBUILD YOUR LIFE How to survive a crisis* (Wheaton, Illinois: Tyndale House Publishers, Inc., 1985), 97.

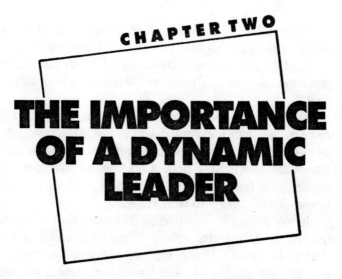

CHAPTER TWO

THE IMPORTANCE OF A DYNAMIC LEADER

*Whatever the Lord says to me, that I will
speak.* 1 Kings 22:14

Al got into his car and began to drive. He had never known such darkness. It was more than the darkness of Portland's night sky. It was the darkness of betrayal and desertion, the darkness of a broken heart. His wife had just left him for another man. Suicide seemed the only answer.

As he continued down the freeway, suddenly he spotted a lighted cross on the hill to his left, rising 100 feet into the sky. Feeling a faint spark of hope, he turned onto the freeway exit and followed the cross.

That magnificent cross might never have become a reality if Dale Galloway had not obeyed the vision God gave him. While planning the construction of New Hope's present 3,000-seat facility, Dale told the architect that he wanted a 100-foot, free-standing, illuminated cross rising high above the building.

"Impossible," the architect informed him. "It's too windy up here on this hill. It simply can't be done."

"But it must be done," Dale insisted. "God has already given me the vision. Therefore, there has to be a way to do it."

Finally, when Dale refused to pay the architect any more money until a way was found to install the cross, the architect came up with a plan. It worked. The cross now stands tall above New Hope Community Church, easily visible from the busy freeway and huge shopping mall below, drawing many to New Hope.

It was a Tuesday night when Al turned his car off the freeway to follow that cross. When he arrived at the church, he found a sizable meeting going on—a meeting for Christian singles. He was warmly welcomed, and sat down to join them. By the end of the meeting, he knew he'd found a reason to live. When the leader of the group gave an invitation to receive Christ, Al opened his heart gladly and became a member of God's family.

The New Hope people opened their hearts to Al, as well. They immediately got him involved in different aspects of the life of the church, loved him, watched over him and encouraged him. Today Al can be found at New Hope praying for and ministering to others who are experiencing the brokenness that he understands so well.

How important is it for the leadership of a church to be obedient to the vision God has given them? Ask Al. If not for Dale Galloway's obedience to God's vision, even in the face of those who said it was impossible, Al might not be around to tell his story.

13 Principles of Dynamic Leadership

"Effective ministry begins with effective leadership," says

Dale. "The pastor must be a man of insight and vision, who is not afraid to make decisions and who, in his walk with God, senses and knows the right time to act."[1] According to Dale, there are 13 principles for achieving dynamic leadership.

Principle No. 1—Strong Leadership Is Essential

One lesson the church needs to learn is that leadership is a fulltime job. All church growth experts agree that the primary catalyst for growth in a local church is having a strong pastor who will be the leader. Dale Galloway compares the leadership of a church with that of leading a successful company or business.

"When we look at the successful companies and business in America," he says, "we discover that they have a board of directors. The board, made up of part-time consultants, will meet once, twice, four times a year to act as wise advisors and thinkers. When they meet they talk about major propositions that their leader presents. They are the counselors who evaluate the leader's ideas before he goes ahead and launches them. When they approve the idea, then their leader, whom they have hired, follows through with making it happen.

"In such cases, who is the leader? Leadership does not rest with the board of directors composed of people who meet for a few hours once in a while. The real leadership rests in the hands of a fulltime executive who has been hired by the board to think ahead, present plans and then carry those plans into action that translates into profit for the entire organization."

Through obedience to the dream that God has given him, Dale Galloway has shown himself to be that type of leader.

Principle No. 2—Be a Balanced Leader

A *task leader* is someone who has a clear-cut vision. With a well-defined goal, the task leader advances in singleness of mind, always finding a way around each and every obstacle. A *cohesive leader* is a lover of people. He will do anything to bring unity, peace and love. He is sensitive to what is going on in other people's lives. To be successful, a church must have a leader who is both a task leader with a clear-cut vision and a cohesive leader who loves people.

Although Dale Galloway is a strong task leader with a clear-cut vision, he is not blinded to his need to be a cohesive leader. Always striving to reach the goals God has given him, he still takes the time to stop and love people. "Every dynamic leader must have a vision," Dale says, "but not tunnel vision. A tunnel-visioned leader will probably reach his goal, but may leave half of his flock behind, bruised, battered and bleeding."

Principle No. 3—Lead with Love

You must earn the right to lead people by the way you love them. People must always take priority over programs. Take time to find out what is going on in people's lives. Minister to them. In Christ's love make them whole. Then they'll be ready to serve the Lord with enthusiasm.

General Eisenhower is reported to have said, "You do not lead by hitting people over the head. Any fool can do that, but it is usually called assault, not leadership."

Pastor Galloway agrees. "A strong leader must be careful not to run people into the ground with high-powered programs. Loving people is always more important than having your own way."

Principle No. 4—Know Who You Are

Don't get caught in the depressing comparison game or

the self-destructive copycat game. Thank God for the way He has made you, the gifts He has given to you, and develop your leadership potential to the fullest. Knowing who you are means also knowing who your church is. What is the calling, the message, the ministry of your church? Who are the people you are trying to reach? What are your objectives? What are your beliefs? What are your strengths? Your weaknesses? Only when you as a leader know who you are and who your church is can you strive to become the best at what God has called you to be.

"If the leadership of a church does not know who that church is," cautions Dale, "then the larger it becomes, the more pressure there is from new people coming in to push the church all over the map. People who come from other churches already have certain mind-sets as to what the church should be.

"Every person on a church staff must work within the context of who that church is. Also, every staff person must be loyal to the senior pastor and support his style of ministry. You cannot have people going off in all different directions doing their own things, and build a great church.

"Recently I had to ask a strong task leader to leave our church because of a conflicting style of ministry. I was not comfortable with that style nor were the members of my staff. We have developed over the years a New Hope-style of ministry. Men and women on staff understand this and work within that circle. I give them all kinds of freedom, wanting them to be themselves, but at the same time expecting them to be an extension of my style of ministry.

"The common bonding factor at New Hope is respect and love for one another. It is very important that a church knows who they are and then works to be the best they can at what God has called them to be."

Excellence in leadership is the ability to set goals and lead people to accomplishing those goals.

Principle No. 5—Set Meaningful and Measurable Goals

A productive leader always sets definite goals and continually measures his progress toward accomplishment of those goals. Every pastor and every assisting pastor on staff needs to set long-range goals, medium-range goals and immediate one-year goals. The tragedy of too many churches is that by not setting goals they aim at nothing and succeed at nothing. Excellence in leadership is the ability to set goals and lead people to accomplishing those goals.

At New Hope, the long-range goal is to have 100,000 members by the year 2000. They know this can be accomplished by growing at a rate of 26 percent each year. Other goals—how many districts, lay pastors and TLC groups to have—are set in accordance with the fulfillment of the long-range goal. Medium-range and immediate one-year goals are constantly being adjusted to meet changing needs.

Principle No. 6—Make the Decisions

A leader is one who can make the right decision at the right time. A leader needs to be in daily fellowship with God in order to be in step with God's perfect timing. A leader must at times be patient and wait for the right hour. At other times he dare not wait but must act quickly. Where possible, seek counsel of those who know the most about the matter at issue, and involve them in the decision-making process. Once a difficult decision has been made, the leader must be able to communicate clearly to his board, pastoral staff, and others the thinking behind the decision.

"In major-league baseball," says Dale, "if a batter gets

a hit one out of three times over a period of seasons, he is a shoo-in for the Hall of Fame. No leader is going to make the right decision every time. But the wise leader does everything he can to keep up his batting average. If you've made a bad decision, admit it and get it straightened out as fast as you can.

"The bottom line is that you cannot be the leader unless you are willing to take responsibility and make decisions at the exact time they need to be made."

Principle No. 7—See and Solve Growth-Restrictive Problems

A leader is one who spots well ahead of time potential problems and sets out to solve them before they strangle church growth. When growth-restrictive problems are solved, a healthy church will naturally grow.

Several years ago, Dale spotted a growth restrictive problem at New Hope. The parking lots were jammed every Sunday. "If people cannot find a parking place," he says, "you've lost them before they have even gotten into the building. We went to work and built an additional 300-car parking lot. The very Sunday that it was completed, we took off on another big growth jump. In the weeks and months that followed, we continued our surging growth because the growth-restrictive barrier had been removed."

Principle No. 8—Be a Communicator

A leader must be a successful salesman. He must communicate the truth as he sees it to his people. When communication is clear, the results are positive. It's the things that people don't understand that produce problems in a church. Dale explains how he used his gift of communication when they were planning their 3,000-seat sanctuary.

"I began with communicating to our entire staff. In response, all of them made financial commitments out of their hearts to our new building. Next I went to the church board and communicated the need for financial commitment. They, too, responded generously by making faith-sized commitments beyond their tithe for the new project. Then we went to a Rendezvous with Destiny committee made up of many of our top givers. Once they grasped the vision and challenge, they responded with commitments to some very large gifts.

"Then we selected and called together our top 400 givers, asking them to serve as a Booster's Club. Almost without exception, each made a financial commitment to our building project. Then, for a four-month period, five mornings a week, I had breakfast with selected members from our congregation at which time I communicated out of my heart about the need for our new building, allowing them to ask any questions and dialogue with me about the project. It was one of the most meaningful times I've ever spent in getting close to a large percentage of our membership.

"We discovered that some of our people could not come at the early morning hour, so we scheduled evening gatherings at which I communicated my heart's concern. We talked back and forth about what New Hope meant to us and about our mission to build a new structure to reach more of the unchurched thousands.

"Then each Sunday over a period of 8 to 10 weeks, one of our lay couples shared a three-minute testimony about the need for the new building and their commitment to it. Along with this, we kept communicating in our weekly publication."

The communication did not stop when the commitments were made. It continued each month through a let-ter mailed to each person who had made a commitment. In those letters were updates on what was happening in the building project, as well as an accounting of the recipient's giving toward the project.

"It has been my experience that whenever communication produces understanding, then you get the positive response from people that you want."

Principle No. 9—Release Lay People for Ministry
There are tremendous numbers of lay people who want desperately to be released for ministry. The clergy must stop protecting their own territory and stifling the work of God and start doing what they have been called to do, which is to make lay people successful in ministry (see Eph. 4:11-13). Learn to trust the Holy Spirit not only to protect your office but to minister through called and chosen lay people. Trusting the Holy Spirit is trusting people to minister.

Pastor Galloway relates a story about a woman in her early thirties, "a mature Christian, dedicated to the cause of Christ. She went to her pastor and presented herself for volunteer ministry on a full-time basis. The senior pastor did not know what to do with her. After she persisted with her offer over several months, he became somewhat irritated with her and delegated her to one of his assistant pastors.

"When she went to the assistant pastor, presenting herself for full-time ministry, he asked, 'What if 50 people came in here, like you, and said they wanted to minister? It would be chaotic. We can't let you run around being a minister. Now, we can use you as a secretary.'

"The woman persisted that she wanted to minister to people. God was calling her to get involved in people's lives: to love them, to pray with them, to win them and disciple them. Sorry to say, the pastors of this particular church were so interested in protecting their own territory that they had no concept of what it means to release lay people for ministry.

"If you will lose yourself to the control and direction of the Holy Spirit, you will find yourself the pastor of a thriving, successful ministry."

Principle No. 10—Use Positive Motivation

A pastor of a growing church will be a motivator, continually encouraging people in the work of ministry. Positive motivation is motivation that stems from love, not fear. It is a proven fact that if people work out of fear, when the boss is away they stop working. But when people work out of love, they serve with enthusiasm (see 2 Tim. 1:7). People will always work harder for recognition, praise and love than they will for any other reward.

"As an individual you have only 168 hours in each week and a limited amount of energy," Dale states. "The only way you can extend and expand your time and leadership is to delegate responsibilities and ministries to others. The more people you have helping you, the more work you can accomplish. Also, other people need to be used. There's a well-known principle that either you use them or you lose them. The person who tries to do everything himself loses all the way around."

Principle No. 11—Make Other People Successful

The way to get your church growing by leaps and bounds is to make other people successful. For every person who becomes successful in ministry in your church, you become that much more successful as the leader and pastor. It is important as the leader that you get so filled with the Holy Spirit, so secure in God's love, so free in being

People will line up to follow a leader, called of God, who knows where he's going, who does everything he can to get people to go with him and who serves God with enthusiasm.

the person God has called you to be that you not only release other people for ministry but do everything you can to make them successful. A growing church will have multitudes of people who are serving and being successful in ministry.

Dale Galloway believes in the old saying, "You can get everything in life you want if you help other people get what they want." He readily admits, "At this point in my life and ministry, I get my greatest satisfaction out of making other people successful."

Principle No. 12—Cultivate and Maintain Good Relationships with Your People

A leader must become a student of human relationships. He must have a sensitivity to the spirit of a person as well as to the spirit of his church. Misunderstandings and ill feelings will do more to stop the flow of power and love and outreach in a church than anything else. The concerned pastor must pay attention to the spirit that exists in relationships.

"Most of the time when an individual is upset with the leader or with the church," Dale explains, "deeper things are going on in their lives than they are talking about on the surface. You've got to be willing to open yourself up and listen so that you can find out what is the problem beneath the surface. Help them get it out. Be an agent of forgiveness and healing and restoration. A leader is one who leads in love and does everything to keep God's healing love flowing in the lives of the people."

Principle No. 13—Serve the Lord with Enthusiasm

No one epitomizes this principle better than Pastor Dale Galloway. Exuberant, excited, encouraging and enthusiastic, he has this to say about serving with enthusiasm.

"There is no calling greater than to be called of God to pastor and lead a church into church growth. A person who has been called of God to do this has a rare privilege and a mighty challenge in life. Be a leader who serves the Lord with enthusiasm. Your enthusiasm will be contagious. People will line up to follow a leader, called of God, who knows where he's going, who does everything he can to get people to go with him and who serves God with enthusiasm" (see Rom. 12:11)[2].

It's Up to You

If a church is to grow, if it is to be effective in ministry and outreach, it must have a dynamic leader at the helm. A pastor who is willing to catch God's vision and commit himself to being obedient to that vision in spite of opposition and seemingly insurmountable obstacles will have a successful church.

NOTES
1. Dale E. Galloway, *20/20 VISION How to Create a Successful Church* (Portland, Oregon: Scott Publishing Co., 1986), 88.
2. Ibid., adapted from 87-99.

CHAPTER THREE

THE POWER OF PRAYER

The effective, fervent prayer of a righteous man avails much. James 5:16

In spite of the beautiful music and the joyful, smiling faces in the congregation, the church seemed huge and impersonal to Donna as she made her way for the first time down one of the long aisles toward the front of the New Hope sanctuary. She was an attractive young woman, neatly dressed—to the casual observer, an average church-goer without a care in the world.

But Donna was not an average church-goer. She hadn't set foot in a church in years. And she had lots of cares; so many, in fact, that she wondered if life was even worth living. She'd heard about God for as long as she could remember, but she didn't really believe that God was in the least bit concerned about her or her problems. If she truly thought He was, she told herself as she slipped quietly into an empty seat, it would make all the difference.

The sermon that Sunday morning was on the power of prayer. As Donna listened, her heart was touched, but she still couldn't imagine what any of it had to do with her. She wondered if she'd made a mistake by listening to one of her neighbors who'd told her, "I hear that New Hope Community Church up on the hill is a real friendly place. Why don't you give it a try?" It had seemed like a good idea at the time. Now, she wasn't so sure.

When others went forward at the end of the service to pray for one another during the time they referred to as the "Garden of Prayer," Donna stayed where she was. I'm sorry, God, she prayed silently, but I just don't have the nerve to go up there by myself. If you really care about me, you're going to have to show me somehow—please!

She'd almost given up hope when, as the Garden of Prayer time ended and the worshipers began to file back down the aisles and out the doors, the young woman who had been sitting beside her stood up to leave. "I don't believe we've met," she said, offering her hand. "I'm Karen."

Donna swallowed the lump in her throat. "I'm Donna," she said softly.

"Did you enjoy the service?" Karen asked.

Donna nodded. "Yes, it was very nice."

"I thought so, too," Karen agreed. "It's good to be reminded of the power and importance of prayer, isn't it?"

Donna nodded again.

"Well, nice meeting you," said Karen, grabbing her purse. "Bye!"

Donna's shoulders slumped and she laid her head in her hands as hot, silent tears spilled down her cheeks. I guess you don't care, God, she thought, because you sure don't seem to be answering my prayers! Maybe it's because I'm just not worth caring about.

*P*eople are praying, the Holy Spirit is working, lives are being changed and God's power is being manifested as those prayers are answered.

And then she felt a hand on her shoulder. She looked up. It was Karen.

"I came back," Karen said. "I was on my way to my car, thinking about what Pastor Galloway had said about prayer, when I realized the Holy Spirit was urging me to come back right away and pray with you." She sat down next to Donna. "Do you feel like talking? Would you like me to pray with you?"

"Yes," Donna whispered. "And I'm so glad you came back! I guess He must care, after all."

Because of Karen's obedience to the Holy Spirit's promptings and her willingness to pray, Donna is now an active part of New Hope Community Church. When Donna realized that the very God of the universe cared about her personally and that He truly does answer prayer, she began to realize her own potential and promise. Another hurt was being healed. Another dream was being born.

People of Prayer

The people at New Hope believe that prayer is the breadth and depth of a Christian life. They also believe that you cannot do God's work without God. That's why prayer is a top priority in the life of New Hope, beginning each day with early morning prayer in the main sanctuary of the church from 6:30 to 7:30. This important prayer thrust is led by the pastors on staff. A weekly prayer night is also held every Friday from 7:00 until 9:00. In addition, hundreds of small groups of New Hope people throughout Portland gather together weekly to pray during their TLC group meetings. In every service at New Hope, there is a Garden of Prayer where people are invited to come together and kneel in prayer and to be prayed for by one of the many lay pastors. Finally, all pastors and leaders of New Hope are expected to model prayer as a way of life.

What happens when believers become people of prayer? Acts 4:31-33 tells us:

1. The place was shaken.
2. They were all filled with the Holy Spirit.
3. They spoke the Word of God with boldness.
4. There was a oneness of heart shared by all of those who had prayed together.
5. There was a sense of stewardship that everything belonged to God and should be used for helping each other.
6. They became winsome, attractive Christians.
7. They ministered with great power.[1]

That is exactly what is happening at New Hope. People are praying, the Holy Spirit is working, lives are being changed, and God's power is being manifested as those prayers are answered.

The Benefits of Prayer

It is prayer that connects us to the power of God. Without the power of the Holy Spirit, we can do nothing (see John 15:5). As we begin to make prayer a top priority in our lives, not only will we see the power of God being manifested, we will obtain countless benefits, including:

- ASSURANCE that personal visions and goals are in line with what God wants;
- STRENGTH and AWARENESS that He is helping us live victoriously and overcome the attacks of Satan;

- CONFIDENCE that the promises we read in the Word are for us;
- WISDOM that surpasses our own. James 1:5 says, "If any of you lacks wisdom, let him ask of God, who gives to all liberally, . . . and it will be given to him";
- CORRECTION when our behavior is not what it should be. This permits our growing into the name "Christian" to continue;
- ATTITUDE changes that need to be made. As we fellowship with the Lord in prayer, there is the renewing of the mind and spirit so important in order to be at our best (see Rom. 12:2);
- CLEANSING when we confess our sins, which renews our fellowship with the Lord and with other Christians (see 1 John 1:9);
- PEACE no matter what goes wrong because we know that Jesus is with us;
- LOVE that frees us so that, through the power of the Spirit within, we can really receive and give love to others;
- JOY, which comes only from the Lord, and is our source of strength.[2]

As David Bryant says in his book *With Concerts of Prayer*, "Prayer is God's frontline way of getting things done."[3] It is God's way of incorporating Christians into His plan of action, His way of allowing us to participate in a miracle.

Learning to Pray Effectively

So how can a church and its members develop an effective prayer life? It's really not that difficult, once we begin to grasp the true meaning of prayer. In *The Real Battle*, Ray

Beeson says, "As we spend time alone with God, we will eventually learn that prayer is much more than just asking God for things and then getting answers. We will learn that the true meaning of prayer is to come into the presence of God himself. . . . It is when we touch him in the quietness of time spent alone with him that the necessary faith for miraculous answers to our prayers is granted."[4]

When the disciples asked Jesus to teach them to pray, He replied with a model for prayer that has become commonly known as The Lord's Prayer (see Matt. 6:9-13). Using that model prayer, Pastor Galloway has come up with the following five-point prayer outline, which he calls the "five fingers on the hand that moves with God" (see fig. 1).

1. *Praise—the Tuning-in Step*
   "Our Father in heaven, hallowed by Your name" (v. 9).
   a. Who He is.
   b. What He has done in scripture and in your life (see Jas. 1:17).

2. *Cooperation—Connection Step*
   "Your kingdom come. Your will be done on earth as it is in heaven" (v. 10).
   a. Pray for God's kingdom to come in your city, in your church and family—every part of your life.
   b. Submit and fit into God's will and leadership in your life (see Rom. 12:1).

3. *Petition—the Receiving Step*
   "Give us this day our daily bread" (v. 11).
   a. Concerns (see Phil. 4:6,7).
   b. Intercession.
   c. Asking for wisdom (see James 1:5).

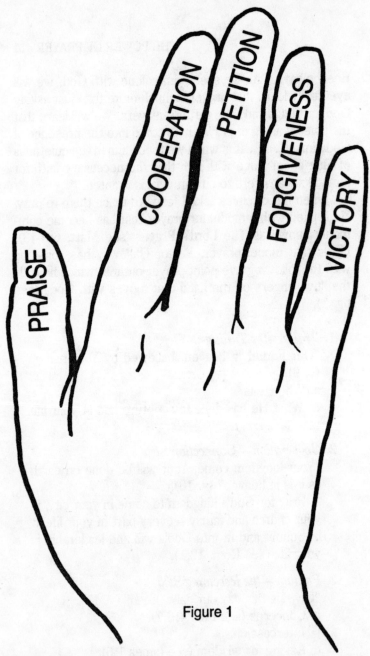

Figure 1

Taken from Dale E. Galloway, *20/20 VISION How to Create a Successful Church* (Portland, Oregon: Scott Publishing Co., 1986), 63. Used by permission.

    d. Praying for and receiving prosperity (see 3 John 2).

    e. Be specific. Detail in steps what you are asking for.

4. *Forgiveness—the Healing Step*
"And forgive us our debts, as we forgive our debtors" (v. 12).

    a. Confession and cleansing (see 1 John 1:9).

    b. Forgiving and blessing those who have wronged you (see Heb. 12:15).

5. *Victory—The Can-Do Step*
"And do not lead us into temptation, but deliver us from the evil one. For Yours is the kingdom and the power and the glory forever. Amen" (v. 13).

    a. Ask for and claim victory over temptation (see Jas. 4:7,8).

    b. In Jesus' name claim deliverance and protection from Satan's attacks (see 1 John 4:4).

    c. Express your desire for God to be glorified in your life.

    d. Make positive affirmations (see Phil. 4:13).[5]

In addition to his five-point prayer outline, Pastor Galloway has discovered ten further helps for effective praying:

1. *Praise and worship*

One way to learn to praise and worship God is through reading the Psalms, which record the prayers of praise (for example, see Ps. 103).

2. *Come clean before the Lord*

If you are to come before the Lord in His holy presence, you must open up in honesty and confession. You must breathe out any wrong attitudes, any wrong motives. You must confess any and all unforgiven sin and breathe in God's forgiveness and cleansing. Before you present your petitions to God, you should make Psalm 19:14 the prayer of your heart:

> *Let the words of my mouth and the*
> *meditation of my heart*
> *Be acceptable in Your sight,*
> *O Lord, my strength and my redeemer.*

3. *Concern*

Learn to share with the Lord the concerns in your life, anything that is causing you anxiety. This may be seemingly impossible projects at work, problems with family or friends, illness, or any number of things. By the time you talk through each concern with the Lord, the muscles in your body, instead of being tight, will become relaxed and at ease. A confidence, assurance, and a strength that is a gift from God will come into your being.

4. *Intercession*

To become an intercessor is to be willing to stand between God and an urgent need, pleading to God in behalf of that need. Abraham interceded for his nephew Lot when God was going to destroy the city of Sodom and Gomorrah. God heard Abraham's cry and saved Lot.

5. *Pray through the day*

In conversation with the Lord, go through the different appointments and plans for your day, asking for His help, guidance and blessing. Ask God to make you a channel through which His love will flow, touch, heal and lift others throughout the day.

6. The "Holy Spirit" Transportation System

The Holy Spirit carries messages from your heart to God, and He carries back from God all that you will need in your life for the day. As you commune with God in this holy fellowship, the fruits of the Spirit are poured into your life: love, joy, peace, patience, kindness, goodness, faithfulness, gentleness and self-control (see Gal. 5:22). These fruits will then become dominant in and through your life because you have become a channel through which the Holy Spirit can communicate the life of the Lord Jesus Christ to others.

7. Be specific

Praying in generalities will not get anything accomplished. How can you even know when your prayers are answered if you just pray in vague, undefined terms? You need to zero in on exactly what it is that you want God to do for you. Your heavenly Father is interested in every detail of your life. He knows how many hairs you have on your head. He knows every need you have. If you have not, it is because you ask not in detail.

8. Be persistent

Should you keep repeating the same request to the Lord? Jesus answered this question by saying, "Ask, and it will be given to you; seek, and you will find; knock, and it will be opened to you" (Luke 11:9). Preceding this verse that teaches the persistence principle, Jesus illustrates the teaching: There was a man who went late at night to his neighbor's house because he needed food to feed unexpected guests. The friend was asleep but because the man persisted in knocking, the friend got up and came to the door and answered his request.

Wherever you find a successful church, a church that is growing phenomenally, a church where miracles happen, where hurts are healed and dreams are built, where people come to allow God to turn their brokenness into blessing, you will find a power center of prayer.

9. *Learn to pray through*
Most of the difficulties we get ourselves into are a result of charging ahead without taking time to really pray through and get God's direction for our lives. We are all a part of the "now" generation. We have instant potatoes, instant TV dinners, instant entertainment, and instant gratification. In order to pray through, you have to be willing to spend a lot of time with God.

10. *Positive prayers*
There is a story about a woman who was having doubts about what God could (or would) do in answer to prayer, so she decided to put Him to the test. She got down on her knees one night and began to pray, "God, if you can hear me, remove that tree outside my window!" On and on she prayed until, as the morning light came softly through the window, she arose and looked outside. "Aha!" she exclaimed. "Just as I thought! It's still there!"[6]

When it comes to getting your prayers answered, asking and thinking are two sides of the same coin. You must ask positively and think positively, cooperating with God to bring the answer you've been seeking. To have God's answers in your life you must cooperate with the power of God (see Jas. 1:5-8).[7]

Power Center of Prayer

Wherever you find a successful church, a church that is growing phenomenally, a church where miracles happen, where hurts are healed and dreams are built, where people come to allow God to turn their brokenness into blessing for others, you will find a power center of prayer. The life of the church will revolve around that power center of prayer. Outreach will grow from that power center. Ministry will begin at that power center. Without it, God's power will not be released in the church. And without God's power, there is no life, no growth, no miracles.

NOTES
1. Dale E. Galloway, *20/20 VISION How to Create a Successful Church* (Portland, Oregon: Scott Publishing Co., 1986), 58.
2. Ibid., adapted from 59-60.
3. David Bryant, *With Concerts of Prayer* (Ventura, California: Regal Books, 1984), 39.
4. Ray Beeson, *The Real Battle* (Wheaton, Illinois: Tyndale House Publishers, 1988), 233, 227-228.
5. Dale E. Galloway, *20/20 VISION How to Create a Successful Church* (Portland, Oregon: Scott Publishing Co., 1986), adapted from 64.
6. Mary Beckwith & Kathi Mills, *A Moment A Day* (Ventura, California: Regal Books, 1988), adapted from 181.
7. Dale E. Galloway, *20/20 VISION How to Create a Successful Church* (Portland, Oregon: Scott Publishing Co., 1986), adapted from 65-70.

CHAPTER FOUR

THE NEED FOR LOVE

For God so loved the world that He gave His only begotten Son. John 3:16

Janet's father died when she was six. Her mother tried to drown her grief in alcohol and men—lots of men—forgetting that her daughter, too, was grieving. Indeed, forgetting about her daughter altogether.

Throughout her childhood and teen years, Janet had difficulty developing and maintaining friendships. What few friends she had, she never brought home with her. She was too ashamed.

By her junior year in high school, Janet was starved for love. Before the year was over, she was pregnant. Her boyfriend talked her into having an abortion. Then he left her. She never went back to school.

Instead, she found a job as a waitress and continued to live with her mother, although the two of them hardly spoke except to argue. When one of her mother's boy-friends raped Janet, she moved out. She didn't report the rape because she figured no one would believe her, including her mother. She also figured she had probably done something to deserve it.

Janet never saw her mother again. By the time her mother died two years later, Janet was so strung out on drugs that she missed the funeral. She was living with boyfriend number five. She had long since lost her job; they supported themselves by selling drugs. Occasionally, Janet sold her favors to one of her boyfriend's buddies. Her boyfriend didn't mind. It was his idea.

When she realized that, once again, she was pregnant, she told her boyfriend. He called her filthy names, refused to accept responsibility for the child, and left.

Once again, Janet was alone. As she had every day of her life since she was six years old, she felt unloved. The pain was more than she could bear. As she drew the razor across her wrists, the only thing she felt was relief.

Janet woke up in the hospital. She had survived her suicide attempt. Her baby had not. She hated herself for having botched the job. She resolved to try again as soon as she was released from the hospital.

Then she met Sharon. Sharon had come into the hospital for some tests. She was assigned to the previously empty bed in Janet's room.

Sharon tried several times to make conversation, but Janet ignored her. The last thing Janet wanted was some talkative roommate! Besides, Sharon was strange. Janet had overheard enough to know that Sharon's tests had to do with cancer. Why wasn't she scared? Why did she seem so cheerful? And why was she always reading that Bible? What in the world could anyone find interesting in a book like that!

That evening, several of Sharon's friends came to visit her. Janet told herself she was glad she didn't have to put up with a bunch of people coming in and bothering her— especially those weirdos! They were just like Sharon— reading their Bibles and talking about God like He was right there with them or something. And people thought she was the one who was crazy—ha!

Janet turned her back to Sharon and her friends and tried to drown out their conversation and Bible reading. It was impossible.

"All things work together for good to those who love God . . . . "[1]

"For God has not given us a spirit of fear, but of power and of love . . . . "[2]

"Behold what manner of love the Father has bestowed on us . . . . "[3]

Love! Love, love, love! Is that all those people ever talked about? Well, maybe the Father had bestowed love on them, but He certainly hadn't on her!

What were they doing now? Good grief, it sounded like they were all praying! Janet turned slowly and peeked behind her. Sharon's visitors stood on each side of her bed. Their eyes were closed. They were taking turns praying for Sharon. As they finished and began to gather up their things to leave, Janet turned away quickly. She didn't want them to know she had been watching—or listening. She certainly didn't want them to think she was interested in any of their crazy God-talk!

"Thanks for coming," called Sharon as they filed out the door.

The last to leave was an older woman in a worn housedress. "Remember," she said, stopping beside Janet's bed and looking back toward Sharon, "Jesus loves you." Her smile was warm as she turned her eyes on Janet. "And He

*The greatest thing in all the world
is to receive God's love and then to
become a transmitter of that love
to others.*

loves you too, young lady!" Then she stepped out the door.

"Wait!" cried Janet.

The woman came back. "Yes, dear?"

Janet's heartbeat was echoing in her ears. She swallowed the lump in her throat and blinked back the hot tears stinging her eyes. "Why did you say that?" she asked.

The woman smiled again and walked over to Janet. "Because it's true," she said, taking Janet's hand. "Because Jesus loves you very, very much."

The tears came then, as Sharon joined her friend at Janet's bedside. Together, they led Janet to Christ, then invited her to their church—New Hope Community.

"It was the first time since I was a very little girl that I really, truly felt loved," Janet said later. "That love changed my life."

Renowned theologian Karl Barth was once asked to sum up the most profound thought he had ever had. His answer?

"Jesus loves me, this I know, for the Bible tells me so." The greatest thing in all the world is to receive God's love and then to become a transmitter of that love to others.[4] It is the stuff that miracles are made of.

What Love Can Do

Dale Galloway insists that the only real secret of New Hope's continued growth is love. "Of all the things that can go on at a church," he states, "love is the greatest."[5] He also says there are six things we need to know about love and what it can do in people's lives.

1. *Love is the most powerful force in the world.*
The great love chapter, 1 Corinthians 13, reveals many

positive facts about God's kind of love. That love is patient, kind, generous, humble, courteous, unselfish, good-tempered, guileless, sincere, edifying (see vv. 4-7). Love is a positive force. Love looks for and finds the best in the other person. One of the key principles of New Hope philosophy is showing positive love through edifying (building up) others. The way to establish a growing church is to get into releasing the positive power of love that God has given.

Pastor Galloway relates a story of a young woman who came into his office to complain about what a terrible husband she had. After listening to her for some time, he asked her, "Does your husband beat you?"

"Oh no," she replied. "He'd never do that."

"Well, does he gamble away the paycheck?" Dale asked. "Does he run around with other women? Does he mistreat you or the kids?"

Each time she answered no, and was becoming indignant with Dale's questioning.

Then Dale asked, "Is he a good father to your children?"

"He's a wonderful father," she answered. "You couldn't ask for a better father."

Dale persisted. "Is he kind and considerate of you?"

The woman smiled a little and said, "He's always kind and considerate of me." She paused a moment, then added, "You know, he's not such a bad person after all! In fact, I'm a whole lot better off than most women."

This woman had forgotten that love is a positive force, that love looks for and finds the best in the other person. As Dale says, "Show me a church where they practice mutual edification and I'll show you a church where the power of love is in action; people will not only flock there, but will stay there."

2. Love is a healing force.

The church is to be God's agent of healing in the broken world. When asked why she came to New Hope rather than some other church, one young lady answered, "Several years ago I came to New Hope but was very mixed up and left and went into a life of sin. For many years I was separated from Christian people, doing my own thing. Recently when I got sick of sin, wanting to come back to God, I went to several churches but did not find acceptance in any of them. Then I came back to New Hope, where people had known me before, and they didn't even ask me about all the stuff in my back yard. They didn't even want to know the details of my sin. All they said was they loved me and we'd go from here, with Christ's help, to make something beautiful out of my life. Here at New Hope Community Church I have found healing love for my broken life." Over the years, thousands of people have found healing and wholeness in the loving atmosphere of acceptance and forgiveness at New Hope.

3. Love is a motivating force.

The Holy Spirit is our motivator. "The love of God has been poured out in our hearts by the Holy Spirit who was given to us" (Rom. 5:5). The more we fellowship with the Holy Spirit, the more we will be motivated by His love within us. To want to love God with all our heart and mind and soul, as He commands us, becomes our greatest desire. Love is the purest, most positive motivation there is. A wise leader will understand well the love motivation of the Holy Spirit and will cooperate with God by appealing to people on that level.

A friend once said to Dale Galloway, "Dale, you're almost fifty years old. You've worked hard all your life. For the last several years, you and Margi have given everything you have to bring New Hope from zero to a church ministering to thousands of people. Why don't you just take it easy, enjoy life?"

Dale's answer? "Because there isn't anything I would rather do than God's work. Having received all of God's love, how can I do less than serve Him with my best? As for me, so long as I live, I will give myself in loving service to God and others."

4. *Love is a unifying force.*

To be successful in the Christian life and in ministry as a church, we really do need each other. It was our Lord's last prayer that we might experience oneness (see John 17). Paul taught that the success of the church was dependent upon its unity and that unity would only become a reality where God's kind of love was being put into practice (see Eph. 4). God' kind of love is a love that overlooks faults and that is led by the Holy Spirit. This love seeks peace one with another. At the same time it respects the uniqueness of each person's calling and spiritual gifts. It helps each person to develop to the fullest in ministry both to the body and outside the church. Love respects each person, honors each person, frees each person. Love gives up selfishness for the good of the whole body. Love never condemns but always seeks to save and restore. Love does not do away with people simply because they do not do what others want them to do. Love respects other people's rights to differ and be different.

This unifying love is evident at New Hope. A church expert once spent a month at New Hope observing, analyzing, and trying to come up with the secrets of what makes it a successful church. One of the principles he cited in his written report was that New Hope Community Church has "unity amidst diversity."

One of the greatest things we can
do for each other in the Christian
community is to affirm God's love
to one another by affirming each
other in love.

What did he mean? He meant that a oneness springing from a deep love for Christ and one another caused them to work together for the good of all and for the accomplishment of the vision God has given them to reach the city of Portland. The members of New Hope are not isolated individuals. They help each other to become so much more than any of them can become on their own. Because of their love, there is synergism, which means there is a miracle of multiplication of abilities as they function together.

5. *Love is a freeing force.*

Most problems in churches arise for the same reason that relationship problems arise in homes, businesses and every place else in society. When people feel insecure and relate out of fear instead of love, anything but good happens. Without the security of love there is bondage and warring both within and without. First John 3:1 tells us, "Behold what manner of love the Father has bestowed on us, that we should be called children of God!" There is no limit to God's love. It is not held back but lavished upon us. Given to us as we are, where we are. One of the greatest things we can do for each other in the Christian community is to affirm God's love to one another by affirming each other in love. Only then will we be truly free to become all that God has called us to be.

Pastor Galloway tells of another church in the Portland area that continues to go through staff people, one after another. What's wrong? "The problem," Dale explains, "is that as talented as the senior pastor is, he feels insecure. Whenever a staff person begins to excel, the senior pastor feels threatened. But a part of his insecurity is that the people expect too much from him. What a difference it would make if the pastor and people would become secure in God's love.

"To be myself frees me as pastor. It frees me to say I have goofed or made a mistake and to ask for forgiveness and to move on in our adventure together. Love forgives, while resentment, hate and anger bind up. So many good people are enslaved to their own feelings. Their ill feelings bind them to the person toward whom they have bad feelings. So many churches are bound up because what they are experienceing and living is not love. Jesus wants to set us free."

6. *Love is a winning force.*
First Corinthians 13 says, "Love never fails" (v.8). In this world we are in a spiritual battle. Either we will be filled with God's Spirit and love, or the evil spirit of destruction will take over in our lives. All the resources of God are ours through the Holy Spirit who lives within us.

One of the lay pastors at New Hope, who happens to be a nurse, gave this testimony: "Today I had an obnoxious patient. I felt like throwing him out the window. But instead, I made the love-choice. I rubbed his back and his feet and was kind and considerate toward him. The payoff came toward the end of the day when his entire attitude changed from hostility to friendship."

Call upon the name of Jesus. Yield to the leadership of the Holy Spirit. No matter what others do. No matter what attack you're under. No matter how unfairly you've been treated. No matter what's going on in your feelings. Make the love-choice because it is the right thing to do. With love you will win, not once, not twice, but again and again. [6]

Practicing Love in an Unlovely World

Practicing God's love in an often unlovely world isn't

always easy. It takes a conscious decision to do the right thing, a concerted effort to follow through. But as we allow the Holy Spirit to rule and reign in our lives, the love will flow. The more we practice that love, the more it will become our way of life. Then, like Sharon and her friends from New Hope, we will be open, comfortable and spontaneous about sharing love with others—others who, like Janet, need that love so desperately. As Janet said, "That love changed my life."

NOTES

1. Romans 8:28.
2. 2 Timothy 1:7.
3. 1 John 3:1.
4. Dale E. Galloway, *20/20 VISION How to Create a Successful Church* (Portland, Oregon: Scott Publishing Co., 1986), adapted from 73.
5. Ibid., 74.
6. Ibid., 75-84.

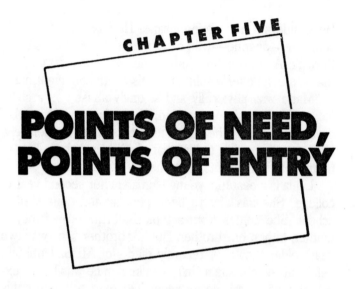

CHAPTER FIVE

POINTS OF NEED, POINTS OF ENTRY

My God shall supply all your need.
Philippians 4:19

The type of needs a church is meeting will directly reflect the type of people that church is attracting. If a church is not attracting any new people, one should wonder exactly what needs are being met, if any. At New Hope Community, the goal is to reach the unchurched. That goal is being realized in a phenomenal way. What is it they are doing that enables them to be so successful where others fail so miserably?

Jerry is an alcoholic. He is 43 years old. His wife finally got fed up and divorced him five years ago. At times he is so drunk he can't remember his ex-wife's name.

Mark functions normally—most of the time. Except when he has flashbacks of his year in Vietnam. He lives in terror of what he might do during one of those flashbacks.

He wonders if he is going insane. He wonders if there is someone—anyone—who can understand what he is going through. And even if he finds someone to understand, can that someone offer a solution to his continuing nightmare?

Maria was physically and sexually abused as a child. Now, although she is married, she refuses to have children, even though her husband wants them desperately. How can she explain to him that she is afraid she will do to them what her parents did to her?

Linda is a beautiful young woman in her second year of college. She has always been popular and done well in school. She comes from a typical all-American family— mother, father, one brother. But her brother, who was two years older than she, recently died—of AIDS. Until just before his death, she hadn't even known he was homosexual. Her parents have forbidden her ever to mention his name to them again. She feels as if she will explode if she can't find someone to talk to soon.

What do Jerry and Mark and Maria and Linda have in common? They're hurting. They have needs. New Hope Community Church is committed to meeting those needs. They also see those needs as potential "points of entry" into the church.

"It takes more than an invitation to a Sunday morning service to get previously unchurched people into church," Pastor Galloway explains. "If we can't offer them something more than what they've already found in the world, if we can't introduce them to Jesus in a way that will minister to them personally, why should they bother to come?"

Jesus always meets people at the point of their need. Thomas couldn't believe in the risen Lord without first seeing the nailprints in Jesus' hands and touching His wounded side. Jesus accommodated him. He met Thomas at the point of his need. Can we be willing to do any less?

These need-oriented, family-type groups are the key to bringing in and keeping new members.

Finding Intimacy in a Large Church

As wonderful as it is to get together on Sunday morning and celebrate the resurrection power of Jesus Christ, it is vital that, throughout the week, the church break down into smaller, more intimate groups, groups designed to develop close relationships and meet needs. Without these smaller, caring groups, it is highly unlikely that many unchurched people will ever set foot in one of the Sunday morning services, much less come back and get actively involved in the life of the church. These need-oriented, family-type groups are the key to bringing in and keeping new members. They are effective, ongoing points of entry into the church.

It is significant that New Hope Community Church is situated across the freeway from the most popular shopping center in Oregon. Dale Galloway, true to his entrepreneur personality, sees people shopping for a church in much the same way they would shop for anything else. "Why is it," he asks, "that so many people pass up several little stores on the way to a large shopping center?" He believes it is because of the vast number of goods and services available in one convenient place. He attributes New Hope's continued growth to that same principle.

And yet, organizing and providing large numbers of need-meeting ministries doesn't just happen. Even a man as dynamic and seemingly tireless as Dale Galloway cannot personally oversee every facet of every activity at New Hope. So, how do they do it?

Organizational Structure

Making use of the Post Office's Zip Code map, New Hope has divided the Portland metropolitan area into four geographical districts, as well as six specialty districts. The six specialty districts are:

- District 21—Positive Singles
  Remarrieds
- District 22—Children's Ministries
- District 23—New Life Victorious
  Prayer and Healing
- District 24—Youth
- District 25—Signs of Love (for the hearing impaired)
- District 26—Women's Ministries

Each of these districts is headed by a district pastor and assistant district pastor, each of whom is directly accountable to the senior pastor. The district pastor, with the help of the assistant district pastor, is over all the members and prospective members living in that district. Directly underneath the district pastor and assistant district pastors are the lay leaders, who are accountable to the district and assistant district pastors, as well as the senior pastor (see fig. 2).

Job Descriptions Within the Structure

The job descriptions for each level of pastor are as follows:

Senior Pastor—The senior pastor is over the entire home cell system. He is continually giving the vision and motivating the district pastors, sectional pastors, and lay pastors in ministry. Through sermons and communications he is actively recruiting lay people into ministry. He sees that they are given the proper training and supervision to be successful. The senior pastor's heart must be in the home cell ministry if that ministry is to be effective. This is

Organizational Plan

Senior Pastor	
District Pastors	
Assistant District Pastors	
Lay Pastor Leaders	
TLC Group Leaders / Lay Pastors	

Taken from New Hope Community Church Lay Pastor Training Manual, 5. Used by permission.

Figure 2

one ministry that cannot be handed over to someone else and forgotten.

District Pastor—This person is either an ordained pastor or licensed assistant pastor with ministerial experience. He or she must reflect stability and be spiritually mature so as to be capable of pastoring a district. Following is a district pastor's job description: (1) Pastor of his/her district, living under the authority of the senior pastor and being loyal and accountable to him/her; (2) Manages the people and assets of his/her district, effectively fulfilling the Great Commission; (3) Develops the lay pastor leaders in his/her district to their greatest potential; (4) Sees that every member of his/her district is discipled and given pastoral care; (5) Leads and causes effective evangelism to happen in his/her district; (6) Has ambitious membership goals and sees that they are met; (7) Works closely with and supervises present lay pastors in order to make them successful; (8) Continues to recruit and motivate new prospective lay pastors into training; (9) Works hard at getting all district members and prospects into TLC groups and has a systematic way to accomplish that goal; (10) Supervises and makes successful the district's TLC groups; (11) Creates new leaders and starts new groups continually in his/her district; (12) Has a strategy for working one-on-one with leaders to extend ministry and make it grow.

Following is an eight-point profile of a district pastor:

1. Leadership—Recruits, motivates, trains; makes others effective in ministry.
2. Evangelism—A soul winner who makes others successful in soul winning.
3. Vision—Has a clear-cut vision for the church and his/her district.

When understanding, caring people are combined with the sort of an organizational structure found at New Hope, then plugged into a church founded on love and a vision from God, it will open up a point of entry for everyone, no matter what their background, their problems, their hang-ups or their lack of previous church background.

4. Love—Is a lover of people.
5. Faith—Believes nothing is impossible with God.
6. Organization and administration—Comes up with an organization that gets the job done in his/her district.
7. Compassion—Has been broken to bless.
8. Enthusiasm—Is a thermostat, not a thermometer.

Assistant District Pastor—This person is appointed by the Senior Pastor and may be either salaried or volunteer to assist the District Pastor in carrying out the responsibilities of the district.

TLC Group Leader/Lay Pastor—On this level, lay leadership begins. Lay pastors are chosen upon completion of the training weekend and three months of visible life of faith. This is reflected in such areas as: consistent attendance in church and TLC meetings; faithfulness in tithing; enthusiasm and wisdom in the Christian walk; having received the fullness of the Holy Spirit.[1]

A Perfect Example

Seventy-five-year-old Helen Lathrop is a perfect example of one of New Hope's broken-to-bless lay pastors. Having three times done battle with cancer, then later being widowed in 1982, Helen knows about trials. But she believes that, with the right attitude toward God, those trials can be used to turn weaknesses into strengths.

When Helen's husband died, she realized that New Hope had no support group for widows. When she mentioned that fact to one of the pastors, she was urged to train as a lay leader and start just such a group. Now, the mutual love and support she and many others have found in that group have given her a new lease on life. "The only difficult times are when you are alone," Helen says. "That's why we all need loving support from others who understand what we're experiencing."

When understanding, caring people like Helen Lathrop are combined with the sort of an organizational structure found at New Hope, then plugged into a church founded on love and a vision from God, it will open up a point of entry for everyone, no matter what their background, their problems, their hang-ups or their lack of previous church background. And people like Jerry and Mark and Maria and Linda will never fall through the cracks of society. They will always have a place to go, a place where they can be sure they will be welcome and their needs will be met.

NOTE
1. Dale E. Galloway, *20/20 VISION How to Create a Successful Church* (Portland, Oregon: Scott Publishing Co., 1986), adapted from 127-129; New Hope Community Church Lay Pastor Training Manual, adapted from 14.

CHAPTER SIX

EVERYBODY NEEDS A LITTLE TLC

Love never fails. 1 Corinthians 13:8

When the grand old patriarch died, children and grandchildren, brothers and sisters, nieces and nephews, friends and neighbors gathered to comfort his widow. They came with cakes and pies and cookies and casseroles, flowers and plants and other expressions of condolences. Everyone seemed to come through the door carrying something.

Except Kevin. Kevin was only four and he wasn't carrying anything when he walked in. His voice quivered as he looked up at his grandma. "I didn't bring you nothin', Grandma," he said, tears forming in his big blue eyes, "'cept my love."

Grandma bent down and put her arms around Kevin. There were tears in her eyes, too. "That's the best gift of all, honey," she assured him. "In fact, it's just what I was needing."

Love. Such a simple word, and yet, so elusive. It's a word we hear every day. We talk about it, sing about it, dream about it. Tragically, so few ever really find it. Many who do cannot seem to hold on to it. Why?

Love is one of the most overused yet misunderstood words in any language. The reason is because when most people use the word love, they are referring to the kind of love that "never has to say you're sorry." Unfortunately, that kind of love only works in the movies. In real life, we need God's love, *agape* love, if we are going to find the kind of love that lasts.

Agape love always puts the other person first. It is a self-sacrificing rather than a self-serving love. And it never happens without commitment.

Growing with Love in a TLC Group

People committed to putting agape love into action are the kind of people you will find at New Hope Community Church. Their primary means for reaching others with this kind of love is their home-cell group ministry, the Tender Loving Care (TLC) groups. A TLC group is a small group of people who "gather in Christ's name and really care for one another. It's belonging and being loved by others. It's being accepted where you are and giving acceptance to other people who come into the circle. It is where heart-to-heart fellowship takes place. It is where the circle of love is continually being enlarged to take in one more person."[1]

An obvious advantage of TLC groups is that the church can grow indefinitely without ever losing the benefits of small-group intimacy. It is also the perfect way to develop effective programs of evangelization and discipleship. New Hope has found at least four ways that TLC groups produce growth:

1. The heart-to-heart fellowship experienced in the TLC group is a different dynamic than in the Sunday celebration services. Participants are no longer members of an audience. They are known and know others by name—giving them a feeling that they are an active part of the Body of Christ.

2. Lay pastors are available for one-on-one care with counsel and prayer about specific needs. Besides being involved directly in evangelism and discipleship, the lay pastors also keep in contact with members who become discouraged for a variety of reasons.

3. Individual spiritual gifts are exercised in building up the Body of Christ and reaching the unsaved community.

4. Weekly Bible lessons are written by the senior pastor, taught by him to the lay pastors and then used in their groups. This systematic study of God's Word is not dependent on a few people who can write and present their own lesson plans. Because the senior pastor has central leadership in the TLC ministry, tremendous unanimity flows through the life of the congregation.[2]

Characteristics of a TLC Group

Besides these four growth-producing benefits, there are 10 basic characteristics associated with TLC groups:

1. *A Close Family*—With thousands of people coming and going in the various services on Sundays, the members from a TLC groups are on the watch for each other. When they find each other in the crowd it's like a family

No church with more than 100 members can be effective in pastoral care without enlisting and enabling the lay people in day-to-day pastoral care.

reunion. There is a deep comradeship of belonging one to the other.

2. *Application of the Bible to Daily Life*—In a TLC group the Bible lesson, which has been taught by either the senior pastor or one of the district pastors in the training session, is given and shared with the people present at the small group fellowship gathering. This format lends itself to feedback and discussion. Questions are asked and dialogue and discussion take place. There is not only the knowledge in the hearing of the Word of God, there is the practical application of it to daily life. Every lesson is both relevant and applicable.

3. *Sharing of Life's Testimony*—An important part of Christian life and growth is the sharing of life through testimony. Recounting one's personal victory in Christ builds up the person sharing as well as those who hear what God has done. As people share their lives and victories with one another, they also get involved in praying for and helping each other. This release of testimony builds great faith and motivates the members of the group to further growth and prayer.

4. *Effective One-on-One Pastoral Care*—The TLC group is an effective way to give one-on-one pastoral care to an unlimited number of people. A steady flow of information from the TLC leaders to the pastoral staff enables the staff to know where and when they need to get involved in back-up ministry. No church with more than 100 members can be effective in pastoral care without enlisting and enabling the lay people in day-to-day pastoral care. New Hope has found that people who never get involved in one of their TLC groups are the ones most likely to leave the church.

5. *Encouragement and Edification*—At one time or another, everyone gets discouraged or down. At the

weekly TLC meetings, members encourage one another. They also continually edify one another. When people are in need of a little personal encouragement, the TLC group is a place to go to have this urgent need met in a beautiful way.

6. *Unlimited Opportunities for Meaningful Service*— The people at New Hope believe that everyone has a desire to serve God in a meaningful way. The TLC groups, with their need for leadership, provide an unequalled opportunity for lay people to participate in meaningful service. Lay people are trained and equipped and released to do the spiritual work of the ministry in the lives of people. In fact, it is not only the lay pastor who is involved in meaningful service in the TLC groups, but each person in the group has the opportunity to minister to another. What brings greater joy to life than to minister to another in Christ's name?

7. *Non-Threatening Friendship Evangelism*—New Hope continually encourages their people to bring to the TLC groups their friends and neighbors and other prospects who have been referred to them. Many people who will not attend a church because it is too threatening will come to a home meeting where they are made to feel welcome and comfortable. Non-Christians brought to TLC groups where they are accepted and included and loved will soon see the love of Jesus in the others and become hungry and thirsty to know Christ. When they are brought to Christ through the home cell group, they are already tied into the group for discipling and care in their newfound faith.

8. *Discipling of New Converts*—New Hope is currently growing at more than 700 new members a year. More than 80 percent of those new members are previously unchurched. In Pastor Galloway's classes for new mem-

bers, about 60 percent of the class consistently stand and receive the Lord Jesus Christ into their lives as personal Savior. There is no possible way to disciple all those new converts without the TLC groups. Once those new converts are established in a TLC group, they will be nurtured in their Christian walk and led into becoming steadfast followers of Jesus.

9. *Spiritual Growth*—TLC groups do not take the place of church attendance. Everyone needs to hear the preaching of the Word, to be a part of the Sunday celebration. However, people who attend New Hope's TLC groups get a substantially larger benefit out of the Sunday services than those who do not attend a TLC group. This is because they are more spiritually alive and in tune with what is happening at the Sunday celebration.

10. *Development of Strong Leadership*—You cannot develop strong leaders by having them sit on the sidelines and watch the pastor do everything. As lay people are used in leading TLC groups, they develop their leadership skills. Taking responsibility, they become responsible. As they are faithful in ministry, their ministry keeps enlarging. As they enjoy successes in leadership, they are prepared for bigger assignments. One of the great things that is taking place at New Hope is the development of hundreds of strong leaders, which promises unlimited potential in years to come.[3]

Starting a TLC Group

The TLC ministry is the heartbeat of New Hope Community Church, as small-group ministry must be in any thriving church. The first thing to do in starting any kind of home-cell group ministry is to designate a leader, an assistant leader, and a host or hostess. Second, decide

An effective three-part formula for starting a TLC group is: build your prospect list, pray your prospect list and work your prospect list.

exactly when and where the group will meet. Then, set the date for the first meeting. This first meeting should be a time of fellowship and getting acquainted. Your goal is to get people to enjoy being with one another and to challenge them to come back each week for the TLC group that is planned.

But where do you find the people? You begin by building a prospect list. Write down anyone and everyone you can think of as a prospective member. At New Hope, prospects are divided by zip codes. List-builders can get names from the proper district pastor, but don't limit your prospects to people in certain geographical districts. If someone from one district seems suited for a TLC group in another district, by all means, encourage that person to join. For instance, one of New Hope's TLC groups is for women with unsaved husbands. Another group is for mothers of deaf children. Obviously, these groups cannot be limited geographically. Group leaders should feel free to invite anyone whom God has laid on their heart. An effective three-part formula for starting a TLC group is: build your prospect list, pray your prospect list and work your prospect list.[4]

What to Look for in TLC Leaders

How can you recognize a potential lay pastor/TLC group leader? Following is an 11-point profile:

1. Has been a producer and a reproducer.
2. Is cooperative and a good team person to work with.
3. Has the time to do the job.
4. High-energy person.
5. Vision for the church's ministry.

6. Gets along well with people.
7. Positive outlook, radiates enthusiasm and maintains good habits in dress and grooming.
8. Growing Christian who models Christianity well.
9. Developing in prayer and fellowship with the Holy Spirit.
10. Shows leadership qualities.
11. Task-oriented.[5]

There are three leadership positions in each of New Hope's TLC groups: the TLC group leader, who must be a lay pastor; the TLC group assistant leader, who must also be a lay pastor or a lay pastor trainee; the TLC group host or hostess.

New Hope has found it helpful to fill all three of these positions in each TLC group, rather than combining the positions. For one thing, it prevents burnout. For another, each position complements the other two. The leader is serving, as well as training an assistant; the assistant is also serving, as well as receiving hands-on training; the host or hostess is then free to serve by offering his or her home for the meetings.

The requirements for a TLC group leader are as follows:

1. Make a home visit and phone call for all prospects, members and friendship card assignments.
2. Work with the host/hostess to make people comfortable.
3. Talk and pray with the assistant leader and host/hostess before each week's meeting.
4. Report to the district pastor each month on the progress of the assistant leader.
5. Initiate the conversational prayer.

6. Lead the Bible lesson and discussion.
7. Be responsible for the report of the TLC meeting (to be turned in at required weekly training meetings and reviewed by sectional and district pastors, as well as the senior pastor).

The requirements for a TLC group assistant leader are:

1. Make a home visit and phone call for all prospects, members and friendship card assignments.
2. Open the meeting.
   a. Introduce guests
   b. Lead the icebreaker activity:
      "Today was a good day because . . . "
      "My favorite color is . . . "
      "My favorite time of day is . . . "
      "One good thing that's happened since last week is . . . "
      "My favorite junk food is . . . "
3. Make any announcements the group needs to know about.
4. Lead the sharing time.
5. Plan the refreshment schedule.
6. Arrange for baby-sitting.
7. Lead the lesson and discussion occasionally on request of the leader.

Requirements for a TLC group Host or Hostess are:

1. With a warm and ready smile, show genuine interest to each guest.
2. Provide a comfortable home (or restaurant/business place).
3. Set up simple refreshments before the meeting

time in order to be ready to greet guests.
4. Arrange chairs in cooperation with the leader.
5. Have extra Bibles and pencils for those who forget theirs.
6. Meet people at the door; show them where to put coats, etc.
7. Set an atmosphere of love and acceptance for everyone—regular attenders and guests—calling them by first names and introducing them to others.
8. Wait until everyone has gone before cleaning up and rearranging furniture.[6]

Besides these requirements, all TLC leaders, assistant leaders, and hosts or hostesses should have the following qualifications:

1. *Enthusiasm*—Enthusiasm is contagious, and a big part of this is working every day toward having a positive attitude. Believe that nothing is impossible with God.

2. *Clear Testimony*—Be able to give a clear, direct witness to what Christ has done within your life.

3. *Dedication*—Dedicate yourself to living by the Bible and being led by the Spirit and dedicated to the Great Commission of reaching the lost. Dedicate yourself to building TLC groups.

4. *Spirit-Led Life*—Be filled with the Holy Spirit and fellowship daily with Him. Effective workers are those who are sensitive to the leadership of the Holy Spirit. An appointed time for daily prayer is a must.

5. *Times and Means*—Group leaders should not be ones who are all bogged down in their own prob-

lems. Be free from bondage in order to serve wholly and effectively.[7]

Suggested Order of TLC Meeting

Following is a suggested order of service for a one-hour TLC group meeting. You can, of course, experiment with other methods until you find the one that works best for you and your group.

1. **Opening (2 minutes):**
   Introduction of guests
   Icebreaker Activity
2. **Opening Prayer (2 minutes)**
3. **Praise (10 minutes):**
   Testimonies
   Singing
   Reports of answered prayer
   Appreciation for each other
   Thanksgiving to God
4. **Conversational Prayer (5-10 minutes)**
5. **Bible Lesson with Practical Application (30 minutes)**
6. **Intercessory Prayer to Make Application of the Lesson (5-10 minutes)**
7. **Closing Prayer (2 minutes)**
   The Lord's Prayer
   Doxology[8]

The important thing about establishing and building an effective home-cell ministry is to start right away by making a commitment to put God's agape love into action. Then, depending on the size of your church, begin with as few as one, two or three small groups. Be patient, pray and expect miracles as your groups grow, divide and multiply, for when you are committed to love, God will definitely give the increase!

NOTES

1. Dale E. Galloway, *20/20 VISION How to Create a Successful Church* (Portland, Oregon: Scott Publishing Co., 1986), 140.
2. Ibid., adapted from 141-142.
3. Ibid., adapted from 142-145.
4. Ibid., adapted from 150.
5. New Hope Community Church Lay Pastor Training Manual, adapted from 12.
6. Dale E. Galloway, *20/20 VISION How to Create a Successful Church* (Portland, Oregon: Scott Publishing Co., 1986), adapted from 147-149; New Hope Community Church Lay Pastor Training Manual, adapted from 21-23.
7. Ibid., adapted from 150-151.
8. Ibid., 151.

CHAPTER SEVEN

JESUS WEPT

*Rejoice with those who rejoice, and weep
with those who weep.* Romans 12:15

A dear lady whose only child had been killed by a drunk driver found her faith in a shambles. Where was the God of love and mercy she had heard about all her life? What kind of a God would take her 12-year-old son from her before he had even had a chance to grow up? Well-meaning friends and loved ones offered words of comfort, such as, "God always takes those at an early age whom He loves most," and "He's better off now, you know; he's with God." The words only made her angrier at God for His seeming injustice.

And then her pastor told her something that melted her anger and bitterness toward God, something that started her back on the road to wholeness and faith once again. "You know," the pastor said softly, "Jesus is crying with you." It had never occurred to her that God had not heartlessly set out to snatch her only child away; rather, that circumstances had conspired to take him from her, and, although her son was indeed safe and happy with God, Jesus' heart was aching as He felt this mother's pain and loss. Realizing this, she was able to reach out to God and accept His love and comfort.

"Jesus wept" (John 11:35). The shortest verse in the Bible, but it says so much. Even though Jesus knew that He was about to raise his friend Lazarus from the dead, He wept. Why? Because His heart ached for Mary and Martha, the sisters of the dead man. Mary and Martha were grieving, they were hurting, they were weeping. Because Jesus loved Mary and Martha, He grieved and hurt and wept with them. And then He rejoiced with them after He had raised Lazarus from the dead.

The Bible tells us in Romans 12:15 that we are to do the same. The pastoral staff at New Hope Community Church, along with the many trained lay pastors, are doing just that. They are reaching out to those whose hearts have been broken by death, divorce, destructive behaviors, abandonment, illness and other tragedies, and they are weeping with them. They are praying with them, ministering to them, encouraging them and rejoicing with them when they experience victories.

New Life Victorious

"I started drinking in high school. I drank for 20 years. Then, a few years ago, I started using cocaine. My wife finally forced me to seek help. That's how I ended up here. I've been sober now for 27 months."

"I'm here because my aunt made me come. She attends church here, and every time I visit her, I come here with her. Now I enjoy it so much I have a hard time choosing which group to attend!"

"I came out of curiosity. I really didn't think I had any problems. Then I began to learn about relationships. It was the first time I had ever really met and recognized the real me!"

"I was an alcoholic for years. One day my pastor saw me crying. He convinced me to come here. I've learned that we do better in a group. By ourselves, we get picked off too easily!"

"I'm here because my daughter brought me. I've learned that part of my healing is getting up and testifying to the power of Jesus Christ in my life."

"I'm a recovering alcoholic and drug addict. I had been seeking treatment for three years, but nothing seemed to work over the long haul. Then I came here. Not only did they offer me an effective program, but they offered me Jesus, too!"

These are just a few of the testimonies given by those attending the many self-help ministries of New Life Victorious (NLV). Based on the 12-step plan that has been so effective for Alcoholics Anonymous, NLV adds a biblical base to the 12-step program, then adapts it to minister to each of the addictive/compulsive behavior groups. Meeting on Monday night, Wednesday morning and Friday night, these groups include alcohol/substance abuse recovery; couples' recovery; family support (co-dependents and enablers); tough love support group; adult children of alcoholics; people who love too much; normal eaters for Jesus; Vietnam vets; restructuring emotional disabilities; women in crisis/victims of rape (emotional, physical, verbal abuse); adult women molested as children; ex-offenders and family support; family and friends of suicide; self-esteem (God's image of you); prayer and healing; positive action for kids (ages 6 through 11 and 12 through 16); learning to love God's way; women who love too much; and more. There is even a class called "Hooked on Life—Not Habits."

"Home-Grown" Ministries

New Life Victorious got its start six years ago when two New Hope members approached Pastor Galloway and said they would like to start a Christian AA group. Dale immediately thought of Betty Jacques. Betty, a recovering alcoholic who had also suffered through the emotional pain of a divorce, had worked at New Hope for several years, first as a volunteer, then as a secretary. She had told Pastor Galloway of her past experiences and of her deep desire to minister healing to others through prayer and support groups. When Dale told her of the two members' request, Betty, a trained lay pastor, agreed to lead the group.

The first meeting of New Life Victorious consisted of Betty's group of six recovering alcoholics. As the group grew, another group was added—substance abuse recovery. After that, a group was started for families of alcoholics. Then a group for people with eating disorders. As a need arose, lay pastors were trained, and more and more groups were started. Betty refers affectionately to these group leaders as "home-grown" ministers.

One of the reasons NLV is so successful, Betty claims, is that Dale Galloway "trusts the Holy Spirit in us." Although lay pastors are trained and supervised, they are also set free to minister. Each lay pastor in NLV is someone who has successfully come through a particular problem and is then trained to help those still struggling with it. It is the broken-to-bless theme in a nutshell. And it works.

"When these people come to us," says Betty, "they are really hurting. Many are members of New Hope, but

We offer them a simple gospel—love, acceptance, forgiveness. And then we stand by them through the long and often painful healing process.

we also get referrals from other churches, from community counseling centers and even from the court system. These people need more than someone telling them they're sinning. They know that, and they already feel bad enough! Many of them have tried for years to change their behavior, only to sink deeper and deeper into despair. We offer them a simple gospel—love, acceptance, forgiveness. And then we stand by them through the long and often painful healing process. Today's society is producing more and more broken, devestated, rejected people. If churches really want to help the sick and the hurting, they are going to have to address this problem."

The Healing Begins
New Life Victorious begins its weekly meetings with a one-hour general session, a time of singing and praising, of giving testimonies to victories gained through the Holy Spirit's healing power within. They then break up into their individual groups where a trained lay pastor leads the others in prayer and discussion.

The alcohol recovery group session is fairly typical of most other group sessions. After an opening prayer, the 12-step program is reviewed, along with accompanying Scriptures. When a new person has joined the group, the others will go out of their way to make him or her feel welcome. First, they will go around their small circle of eight or nine participants, telling a little about themselves in order to put the newcomer at ease.

"I'm Kelly. I've been sober for eight years, but I still have some issues to deal with."

"I'm Dennis. I was sober for two years, but I backslid. So here I am again."

"I'm Chris. I've only been sober for three months, and I'm still having a real hard time."

"I'm Mike. I've been sober for eight months now, and I'm actually holding a job for the first time in my life! It's exciting."

As the lay pastor leads the discussion, a noise is heard in the hallway outside the room. The door handle turns tentatively, but stops. They hear a faint knock. The group leader goes over and opens the door.

"Would you like to join us?" the leader asks.

The dirty, bearded man shrugs, staring down at his worn tennis shoes.

"Please," the leader says encouragingly.

The man steps into the room, his eyes still downcast. The group gives him a warm welcome, pulling up an empty chair for him. He sits down in the chair, his hands clasped tightly under his legs.

"I . . . I can't get my hands to stop shaking," he says, his voice cracking with emotion.

"How long have you been sober?" someone asks.

"Eight days," he whispers. "Eight days out of 20 years. I . . . I don't know if I can make it."

The response is immediate. Everyone knows exactly how he feels. They come to stand around him, laying hands on his shoulders and his back, as the lay pastor begins to pray. Others join in. Tears flow freely. It will be a long, hard road, but the man who has only been sober for eight days in 20 years has finally found the help he has been seeking.

Prayer and Healing

As these recovering alcoholics minister to their new friend, down the hall another group is meeting for prayer and healing of varied needs and problems. This group, part of the prayer and healing ministry of New Hope, is also overseen by Betty Jacques, whose official title is Pastor of New Life Victorious and Prayer and Healing Ministries.

"The New Life Victorious ministries and prayer and healing ministries just go together naturally," she says. "Without prayer and total healing, you can never truly find a new, victorious life."

Betty began her ministry in prayer and healing six years ago, about the same time she began leading the first New Life Victorious group. She and her husband were both trained lay pastors and had led a TLC group for some time. When Dale first approached her to start a class in prayer and healing, she "had no idea how widespread the prayer and healing ministry at New Hope would become." But as busy as the two ministries keep her, it is obvious from her warm, contagious laughter and the sparkle in her eyes that she thrives on her time spent in these two areas.

"What could be more exciting," she asks, "than to see people who have lived their entire lives in bondage to destructive habits finally finding a light at the end of the tunnel? Most of these people have had to use every ounce of their energy just to survive. There was nothing left over for creative development. Now, they have a chance to discover themselves, to see what they can do, what they can become. It's so very rewarding to be able to be a part of it all, to be there to watch the miracles unfold."

Unfold. Softly, carefully, like a rose, one petal at a time. But don't they ever just burst forth all at once? Isn't that how miracles are supposed to happen?

"Once in a great while," Betty explains, "we see a miracle happen all at once, right before our very eyes. And when it does, we all jump up and down and praise the Lord! But that is definitely not the norm. The truth is, most life-changing miracles take time, lots of time. That's why it's so important to do more than just pray once for these people and then turn them loose. They aren't ready to make it on their own yet. They need follow-up prayer and ministry, fellowship and discipling. We have to saturate them with love and acceptance. Their problems have been years in the making. Very seldom are they going to clear up in five minutes."

An Outflow of God's Work from Within

The reason it takes time for total healing to take place, Betty says, is that "healing is actually an *outflow* of the work that God is allowed to do from *within*." In Mark 7:20-23 Jesus says:

> *What comes out of a man, that defiles a man. For from within, out of the heart of men, proceed evil thoughts, adulteries, fornications, murders, thefts, covetousness, wickedness, deceit, licentiousness, an evil eye, blasphemy, pride, foolishness. All these evil things come from within and defile a man.*

Betty bases her prayer and healing ministry on this Scripture. She firmly believes that much of what is within is deeply buried, and can only be rooted out and healed through prayer and the intervention of the Holy Spirit. "Many of us are not even aware of what it was that happened at different points in our lives that cause us to act and react as we do. Sometimes these things happened so long ago that they have faded from our conscious memories. Sometimes the things that happened were so painful, we have purposely chosen to forget them. Either way, they must be remembered and identified as the source of many of our problems. Then, as we allow the love of Jesus

The need for healing is universal, and we want to minister to as wide a spectrum as possible.

to be applied to those areas of pain and sickness, the healing can begin."

The prayer and healing ministry at New Hope was originally referred to as "inner healing" but, because of the negative connotations associated with the use of the term "inner healing" in the New Age movement, it was changed to "total healing," which, according to Betty, is the more accurate term. "Healing must involve the physical, emotional, mental and spiritual realms if it is to be a total, complete healing. These four areas are all inter-related. If one area is sick, they are all affected."

Although Betty readily admits that physicians and secular counselors have had varied degrees of success in healing the physical, emotional and mental areas. "Without Jesus, they can never find healing for the spiritual realm. Therefore, the healing can never be complete."

A Balanced Ministry

New Hope currently has 50 healing-team members working directly under Betty. Every three months they sponsor a "Total Healing" seminar, which lasts 10 hours. The seminars are limited to 150 people. It is an intense 10-hour seminar, and interested people must sign up early.

"We try to keep abreast of what is going on in the healing ministries," Betty says. "But we also try to balance the ministry so that we can help as many people as possible. We've studied the healing techniques used by the Pentecostal/Charismatic denominations, as well as the conservative denominations. We don't want to turn people off or scare them away. If someone is comfortable with a certain type of prayer, we use it. If not, we don't. The need for healing is universal, and we want to minister to as wide a spectrum as possible."

Betty, who is licensed as a minister by the state of

Oregon, is presently working toward her ordination. During the six years she has served in her capacity with New Life Victorious and the prayer and healing ministries, she has seen phenomenal growth, both in individuals as well as in the ministries themselves.

"It's exciting to see how many men are now involved in New Life and prayer and healing. When we first started the seminars, it was all women. Now it's fifty-fifty. We have people of all ages, from all walks of life, representing all sorts of needs. Just when we think we've heard every story possible, in walks someone new with a different need than any we've come across yet. But, praise the Lord, we serve a God who understands us, a God who cries with us, and a God who is big enough to take care of each and every one of our needs!"

CHAPTER EIGHT

A MINISTRY FOR EVERYONE

*Now there are diversities of gifts, but the
same Spirit. There are differences of
ministries, but the same Lord. And there are
diversities of activities, but it is the same
God who works all in all.* 1 Corinthians 12:4-6

John and Mary have been married for 37 years. Their children are grown and doing well. Their grandchildren are adorable. Recently retired, their latter years are turning out to be all they had expected. With everything so rosy, what could New Hope possibly have to offer them?

Sally and Don have recently married. It is the second marriage for both of them. Sally had two children from her first marriage, Don had none. Can New Hope meet the needs of this blended family?

And what about Jim? Jim is 30, unmarried, and very involved in his career. He has never had a problem with drugs or alcohol, his childhood was pleasant, his relationship with his parents is positive. But there is an emptiness within him, a void calling out to be filled. Can New Hope help him identify and fill that void in his life?

Kathleen was widowed at a young age, but managed to raise her two children while going back to school and pursuing a career. Now a successful businesswoman, what reasons could she have for attending New Hope?

Chuck's needs seem fairly obvious. His wife and infant son were recently killed in an automobile accident. He was driving. The grief and guilt are overwhelming. Can New Hope help him survive and recover from his crushing loss?

Sherry is 45 years old. Three of her four children are grown, two of them still in college. She and her husband had been active in their small church for more than 20 years. When her husband suddenly announced that he was leaving her for a younger woman, Sherry was devastated. How could this be? Divorce doesn't happen to Christians—does it? Her pastor was sympathetic, but could offer her no more than a prayer and an encouraging word. He had never walked in her shoes. Few people in their small church had. Sherry needed more. Someone told her about New Hope. Could this be the answer she was looking for? Was there someone there who understood her pain, her rejection, her feelings of helplessness and hopelessness?

Different people with different needs. Some of them are not even aware that they have a need. Others sense only vaguely that something is missing in their lives. But everyone, everywhere, has some sort of need. That's what the people at New Hope believe, and that's what they contend with on a daily basis. Whether the problem is catastrophic and desperate, or a seemingly minor one caused by the common stresses and strains of everyday living, New Hope believes that the love of God, working through the people of God, is the answer. They believe that, because the Bible says:

*No temptation has overtaken you except such
as is common to man; but God is faithful, who
will not allow you to be tempted beyond what you
are able, but with the temptation will also make
the way of escape, that you may be able to bear it*
(1 Cor. 10:13).

God is bigger than any problem anyone will ever face.
He is aware of the problem before it happens, and He
already has the solution. Therefore, it is possible to minister to people in any given situation, so long as those ministering are able, through some personal experience, to
relate to those in pain, and so long as they remember that
it is only God's love working in and through them that will
help and heal and restore. On that premise, New Hope
seeks to establish a ministry to fit the needs of anyone and
everyone who walks through their doors.

Women's Ministries

Although Dale Galloway sees himself as the visionary, the
goal-setter at New Hope, he readily admits that his wife,
Margi, is the "people person."

"There is a lot of crossover in our relationship and our
ministries," says Dale. "We are both strong leaders and
we occasionally butt heads, but I wouldn't be where I am
or who I am without Margi. She's the one who brings the
spark and the enthusiasm to New Hope."

Margi Galloway, a perky, attractive blonde with a beautiful singing voice, explains, "I love music and I enjoy very
much working in the music ministry. But I have a heart for
women. Women can make or break a church. It is vital to
keep women positive, motivated, busy, contributing.
That's the reason I work so hard as head of women's min-

istries here at New Hope. I see myself as an encourager, a self-esteem builder. I want to see the women I pastor be successful."

Margi Galloway's hard work is paying off. Women's TLC groups are constantly expanding and multiplying. Their annual women's retreat is a continual success, as are their mother/daughter luncheons, monthly women's fellowship meetings and periodic workshops. "We believe we should provide enough variety in the women's ministries that every woman who walks into our fellowship will find one or more slots perfectly suited to her needs. This includes women who are married, single, separated, divorced or widowed; young, middle-aged or seniors; mothers or grandmothers of toddlers or teenagers; homemakers, career women; women in need of ministry and those with a desire to minister to others."

One of the larger and very active women's groups at New Hope is known as MOPS (Mothers of PreSchoolers). MOPS is a "program for young mothers of children under school age, infant through kindergarten. In this high-stress period of a mother's life she often feels inadequate, frustrated, isolated or lonely. Frequently these feelings go unresolved. MOPS shows care in meeting significant needs of the woman by: providing for the development of close friendships; motivating innate creativity; promoting spiritual growth. The MOPS format includes regular group meetings with instruction relating to womanhood, marriage, child rearing and family relationships, given from the biblical perspective. Small discussion groups provide for honest sharing, deepening friendships and spiritual enrichment. A craft time stimulates creative expression, self-confidence and a sense of accomplishment."[1]

While these young mothers are meeting every first and third Tuesday of every month from 9:00 until 11:30

To be successful in any ministry you must first have a sincere, unconditional love for people —all people.

A.M., their preschoolers are being loved and cared for through the ministry of MOPPETS, a time of structured activity geared toward contributing to the young child's social, physical, creative and spiritual development.

Noted author, speaker and clinical psychologist Dr. James Dobson has this to say about New Hope's MOPS and MOPPETS ministries: "I am very concerned about the isolation of the mothers of small children. I respect and appreciate so much what you are doing."[2]

A Christian aerobics class called Fitstop is another activity offered through the women's ministries. Morning and evening classes are scheduled throughout the week, and baby-sitting is provided. Their motto? "All 'Body Conditions' Welcome!" Their goal? "A better you!"

There is also a TLC group for mothers of deaf children, as well as a group for women with unsaved husbands. Although the existing list of women's ministries is finite only because it is limited to those needs which, to date, have been identified, Margi believes the possibilities for expansion of those ministries are endless.

"As a new need surfaces, God will provide us with a new ministry to meet that need," Margi states emphatically. "Above all, I believe that to be successful in any ministry you must first have a sincere, unconditional love for people—all people. That love, of course, can only happen when you have cultivated a deep and unconditional love relationship with Jesus Christ."

Men's Ministries

The men at New Hope are also very active. With seven TLC groups meeting in different locations and at different times of the day or evening, there is a group for everyone, wherever they live, whatever their time schedule. In addition to the TLC groups, a men's monthly fellowship breakfast is held on the first Saturday morning of each month in New Hope's fireside room.

The monthly fellowship breakfasts are an outreach to the community, as well as a time of celebration for all the men's TLC groups, which have been meeting throughout the month in local restaurants and business locations. Along with enthusiastic music and praise, these Saturday morning events feature special speakers with a strong Christian witness, who are inspiring as well as enlightening on a particular area of professional expertise.

The men's fellowship recently began an exciting project of providing scholarship funding for a sixth grade catechism within New Hope, as well as reaching out to and including other area churches. The money is raised for this ministry by hosting an annual Northwest Christian artists' benefit concert for aspiring groups or individuals seeking to glorify God with music and to gain exposure to the community.

Another direct benefit of this low-cost admission concert is the supplying of New Hope's food storage cupboard. Those attending the concert bring a non-perishable food item along with their purchased tickets.

Annually, the men's fellowship holds a men's retreat or an all-day men's spectacular event hosting speakers and workshops of special interest to men seeking personal growth in various areas of their lives.

The men's fellowship of New Hope Community Church is dedicated to building strong Christian families by building strong Christian men. They believe that, by lifting up the name of Jesus before men through the weekly TLC groups and the monthly fellowship breakfasts, men will grow in their knowledge and practical application of loving and leading God's way.

Other Adult Ministries

All adults, for one reason or another, are classified as either married or single. At New Hope, there is a ministry designed to fit each and every one of them.

New Hope's Positive Singles' ministries, led by Pastor Rich Kraljev, publishes their own newsletter, *Single Review*, which combines uplifting, inspirational articles from Pastor Kraljev and others, occasional interviews or profiles of New Hope singles and announcements of upcoming events. Some of the singles activities include TLC groups, sports, seminars, workshops, retreats, game nights and potlucks. Singles groups are also divided according to ages.

Many who attend the singles activities are also involved in one or more of the other adult ministries, which include separation survival, divorce recovery, positive parenting and grief recovery. One active participant in many of the singles ministries is Judy Kennedy, one of the district pastors at New Hope.

Having survived both divorce and widowhood, Judy says there were times she thought her "night of weeping would never end." But through her pain, as she was forced to walk the long road back to wholeness—not once, but twice—she has learned the importance of clinging tightly to the Lord, as well as finding a support network of people who care and understand. "That's what's so wonderful about New Hope. There are people here who love the Lord and each other, who understand and reach out to those in pain."

And what about those adults who are not single? Do all married adults fit into the same slots, have the same problems, the same needs, the same goals and dreams? Hardly. New Hope recognizes that. There are groups for young marrieds, for remarrieds, for engaged couples, as well as groups to improve positive parenting skills. In short, married or single, there is at least one group for each and every adult at New Hope.

Children's/Youth Ministries

Children and youth of any age will never find themselves without something to do at New Hope. Clara Olson, New Hope's Children's District Pastor, sees their children's program as having two main goals: to minister to the child, and to be a strong support system to the parents. A warm, charming lady with an obvious love for children, Clara heads up a children's department that encompasses countless programs for children and their parents, including:

Nursery—Professionally staffed to care for infants through 3-year-olds on Sunday mornings and evenings, as well as five evenings during the week and daytime activities at the church.

Sunday School—During each Sunday morning service, classes are held for 2-year-olds through sixth grade. Professionally trained teachers.

Special Education Class—During each Sunday morning service, a class is held for handicapped children.

Children's Celebration—During second Sunday morning service for children grades 1-6 who have already attended Sunday School in the early service. Songs, prayer, stories, movie, video, evangelistic thrust.

Mailbox Club—Home study lessons for children in grades 1-6. Children may join this club upon request or are automatically enrolled when they place their faith in Jesus as Savior during Sunday School or Children's Celebration.

Children's TLC Groups by Geographical Districts—
Loving support groups where children ages 4-12 learn and
grow together. Meet in homes throughout city. Led by lay
pastors.

Friendship Big Brother/Big Sister Program—Provides
a companion and friend for children who need strong
Christian role models and additional adult support in their
lives.

Children's Rallies—Conducted quarterly. Fun, educa-
tional, entertaining. Designed to give children the opportunity to invite their friends to church. Guest speakers,
music, movies, activities, puppet shows, outreach.

Children's Camps—For grades 1-3 and 4-6. Three to
four days out of the summer for each age group. Fun,
adventure, crafts, sports, worship, music, new friends,
live in cabins on the grounds with other children their age
and also their counselors.

Vacation Bible School—A five-day summer outreach
Christian education program. Delights children nursery-
sixth grade with Bible-learning activities, music, memori-
zation and opportunities for spiritual and social development.

"I Believe" Class—Theological class designed especially for sixth graders. Includes a variety of assignments
and Scriptures to give children a solid foundation for their
faith at this strategic time in their lives. Introduction class
on a Saturday in the summer, followed by a three-day
beach retreat with more classes and fun. Ends with children choosing to become members of the church and
being baptized on the Sunday following the retreat. [3]

In addition to these and other children's programs, the
junior high group, led by Pastor Bob Kavanaugh, is consid-
ered by the kids who attend to be the "raddest place

around!" Coming from a junior higher, that is the *ultimate* compliment.

There are a variety of programs at New Hope for the junior higher. The Sunday School program includes worship and two morning services centered on strong biblical principles and prayer. "Lifeguard" is a discipleship program designed to help kids dive deeper into God's Word, as well as go out and invite other kids to their youth group. There is also an active youth choir where junior highers can learn to praise the Lord through singing. On Wednesday evenings, the junior high group meets for music, skits and group discussions focusing on life's everyday problems. "Praisin' Players" is a group that uses the power of drama with a spiritual basis to reach out to the youth in the community. "Common Ground" is a support group for youth affected by parental divorce.

Sold Out and Radical (SOAR) is the high school group, led by Pastor Jack Shumate. In addition to youth revival nights, retreats, sports and weekly meetings, SOAR, along with the junior highers, has youth TLC support groups. Many of these youth are trained in lay ministry, and work not only with other youth at New Hope but organize and lead Bible studies on their school campuses, as well.

Pastors Kavanaugh and Shumate have outlined five foundational principles on which they base their youth ministries. They are:

1. *Cell (TLC) Groups*—Young people need individualized attention to their needs. This is step #1 toward effective discipleship. *This is not an option.*
2. *Ownership and Vision*—Without ownership or a vision, the program will falter and spiritual growth will fade away.

What kids are really looking for is the truth. If we're phony, they'll see right through us.

3. *Each One Bring One*—Growth through multiplication, winning non-Christian friends.
4. *Common Ground*—Find the common ground and meet them there. This provides unity; i.e., being spiritual to a teen is different from being spiritual to an adult.
5. *Top to Bottom*—Everything starts at the top and works its way to the bottom (2 Tim. 2:2).[4]

One thing both youth pastors agree on is, "What kids are really looking for is the truth. If we're phony, they'll see right through us."

Both pastors insist their programs are more than glorified baby-sitting for teens. "It's not enough just to keep them busy," Pastor Shumate explains. "Our activities have to be meaningful. We only have these kids for a short time every week. Most of them come in here with some serious needs. We don't want them to leave as empty as they came."

Miscellaneous Ministries

New Hope Community Church offers opportunities for ministry to all ages. For those who are musically inclined, there are orchestras and choirs for children; youth; singles; young, middle-aged or senior adults. For deaf youth and adults, there are Sunday School classes; signing during the second Sunday morning service as well as other services during the week; TLC groups; and two-year classes in sign language. An active, lively seniors group keeps those in their golden years feeling useful and fulfilled. A relationship class, led by a husband/wife team, specializes in teaching men and women how to form lasting, meaningful friendships. A writer's guild exists to help and encourage those who have literary talents and aspirations. The list of New Hope ministries is never complete, because it is always growing.

Is there a place for everyone at a church like New Hope? A place for John and Mary, for Sally and Don, for Jim, for Kathleen, for Chuck, for Sherry? Yes, because New Hope recognizes and respects everyone as individuals, realizing that no two individuals are alike; therefore, no two individuals have the exact same needs. All of their needs, however, are legitimate, and every effort must be made to meet those needs if the church is to accomplish the purpose for which it has been called, if it is to be an effective agent of love and healing in an ever-changing, yet ever-suffering world.

NOTES

1. MOPS information pamphlet, New Hope Community Church.
2. Ibid.
3. Adapted from children's ministries information pamphlet, New Hope Community Church.
4. Adapted from youth information folder, New Hope Community Church, p.1.

CHAPTER NINE

SO, NOW WHAT?

And He Himself gave some to be apostles,
some prophets, some evangelists, and some
pastors and teachers, for the equipping of the
saints for the work of ministry, for the
edifying of the body of Christ.
Ephesians 4:11,12

We've talked a lot about the phenomenal success and growth of New Hope Community Church. We've met several of its members. We've eavesdropped on some of their meetings. We've discussed the love, the acceptance, the prayers, the needs, the programs, and especially the concept of the home cell (TLC) groups led by trained lay pastors. So, now what? How can you benefit from what New Hope is doing? How can you start a lay pastor ministry in your own church, a ministry that will be effective in reaching out into your community to meet needs, heal hurts and build dreams?

What Is a Lay Pastor?

First, what is a lay pastor? According to Dale Galloway, "A lay pastor is a person who has answered the call from God to do the work of ministry."[1] At New Hope, lay pastors are given permission to do the same things as do the paid staff pastors, limited only by the amount of time they have to give. The lay pastor program is adjusted to fit the time requirements of those involved.

New Hope sees the work of a lay pastor as being four-fold: missionary (see Matt. 28:18-20); ambassador for Christ (see 2 Cor. 5:19,20); shepherd (see John 21:15-17); servant (see Rom. 12:1 and Matt. 20:28). They divide their lay pastors into four levels:

1. *Lay pastor trainee*—This is where everyone begins. For the first 90 days each one enters the lay pastor ministry as a lay pastor trainee. During this time, trainees are expected to attend weekly training meetings for continuing supervision and training. They are expected to begin to take an active part in the ministry, beginning where they are and moving to where they want to go. They are closely supervised by the district pastor and sectional pastor. At the end of the 90 days, if the person in training has proven to be faithful in ministry, then, in a public ceremony, he or she is awarded the lay pastor badge. These badges are worn with pride and a sense of responsibility to carry out the work of a lay pastor.

The requirements of a lay pastor trainee are:

- Committed to Christ and wanting Him to be Number One in his/her life;
- A member of the church;
- Completes the weekend of lay pastor training;
- Passes lay pastor written examination;
- Accepts an assignment as leader or assistant leader of a TLC group;
- Approved by pastoral staff;

- Regularly attends the weekly lay pastor's training meetings;
- Gives a written report each week for personal ministry;
- Is faithful in attendance at the worship services of the church;
- Is faithful in tithing to the Lord's work.

2. *Lay pastor*—The lay pastor really becomes the arms and legs of Jesus Christ in the church, reaching out, touching people within the body and beyond, taking them into the very presence of Jesus. The requirements of a lay pastor are:

- Serves as a lay pastor trainee for at least three months;
- Accepts an assignment as leader or assistant leader of a TLC group;
- Regularly attends the weekly lay pastor's training meetings;
- Gives a written report each week for personal ministry;
- Is faithful in attendance at the worship services of the church;
- Is faithful in tithing to the Lord's work;
- Follows up on assigned Friendship Cards.

3. *Senior lay pastor*—This is a person who has proven faithful and who has walked with the Lord in ministry over a two-year period. This person's life has, in turn, reproduced the fruits of additional lay pastors and other TLC groups. The position of senior lay pastor is a very special level of ministry. The requirements of a senior lay pastor are:

- At least two years of continuous faithful service;
- Faithful attendance in all of the lay pastor events;
- Follow-up on assigned Friendship Cards;
- Successful leadership in TLC groups;
- Impeccable moral life, biblically grounded;
- History of humility and faithfulness to Jesus, church and pastoral staff;
- Consistent tithing record;
- Solid family life—this applies both to a single family as well as a married family.

4. *Lay pastor leader*—The fourth level in the lay pastor program is that of lay pastor leader. The requirements of a lay pastor leader are:

- Faithful ministry as a lay pastor;
- Reproduces other TLC groups from his/her own TLC group;
- Recruits new lay pastors, which he/she then supervises and makes successful;
- Accepts assignment from his/her district pastor of supervising other lay pastors;
- Signs a written commitment to ministry for a one-year time period;
- Is selected by his/her district pastor and approved by senior pastor;
- Gives a written report to his/her district pastor on the progress of each of the lay pastors being supervised.[2]

What Is Expected of a Lay Pastor?

New Hope has 12 basic expectations and requirements for lay pastors, which are:

1. To be consistent and committed in living the Christian life-style, with a daily commitment to prayer as a top priority;
2. To see the vision of New Hope Community Church and be loyal to its leadership, and committed to accomplishing the great things that God has called them to do;
3. To be dependable and accountable to those placed in leadership;
4. To be led and controlled by the Holy Spirit;
5. To be a regular participant in a TLC group, either by leading a group, or by assisting in the leadership of that group;
6. To attend a weekly lay pastors' meeting, scheduled at three different times during the week;
7. To wear the lay pastor's badge each Sunday, and to be sensitive and respond to the needs of those attending the service;
8. To come to the Garden of Prayer during Sunday services and pray for those who have come forward;
9. To work faithfully and diligently each week in doing what God has called them to do;
10. To be a member of New Hope Community Church, complete the special lay pastor training and pass a written exam, and be selected by the pastoral staff;
11. To be faithful in tithing and giving time;
12. To maintain a solid family life.[3]

Advancement and Accountability

Dale Galloway believes that "One of the weaknesses of most churches is that there is no opportunity for lay peo-

One of the weaknesses of most churches is that there is no opportunity for lay people to advance in ministry.

ple to advance in ministry. God has created us with a need to reach for new levels of attainment."[4] The opportunity for advancement is part of New Hope's lay pastor program. Even a senior lay pastor has the opportunity to become a sectional pastor and even a district pastor.

At the same time, if a lay pastor ministry is to be effective, "people must be held accountable for what they have committed themselves to do."[5] On occasion, loving discipline is called for, based on the following statements taken from the lay pastor training manual:

Discipline for More Effective Ministry

1. Each person who is in the lay pastor ministry will be accountable to:

   a. Senior pastor;
   b. District pastor.

2. A person in the lay pastor ministry may be disciplined for any of the following reasons:

   a. Not carrying out the ministry assignment that was accepted;
   b. Not attending the weekly training meeting;
   c. Any kind of immorality;
   d. Any spirit of bitterness, disloyalty, or strife that causes harm to other people in the church;
   e. Teaching false doctrines.

Procedure for Discipline

1. The discipline will vary from a loving and prayerful talk with the district pastor to the point of asking the person to step out of the lay pastor program for a given period of time;

2. If the district pastor requests it, the lay pastor badge will be surrendered;

3. All discipline will have as its goal the redemption and restoration of the individual as well as the good of the Body of Christ.[6]

How to Train Lay Pastors

Three times a year, from Wednesday through Saturday of the first weeks in October, February and May, New Hope has what they refer to as a "Lay Pastor Super Bowl." For six weeks beforehand, through sermons and church communications, they recruit people to come to the Super Bowl to become lay pastor trainees. On the first day of the Super Bowl, they invite all of the lay pastors to come in to help get the new trainees off to a good start, as well as to rejuvenate and make successful the present group of lay pastors. By the second day, they have laid down all the qualifications and basic training for being a lay pastor. The Super Bowl is concluded by having everyone who wants to become a lay pastor in training to sign a lay pastor commitment sheet. *The Super Bowls are open to anyone, regardless of church affiliation or geographical location, although pre-registration is required.*

New Hope's lay pastor trainees also meet one-on-one with their district pastors to spell out exactly how the new lay pastors will begin ministry. Nothing is left to chance. If a person is going to be a lay pastor in training, he or she must become involved in ministry. There are no free rides.

Every lay pastor from any of the four levels is expected to be at one of three weekly training sessions. At this training session, each one is to turn in a lay pastor weekly report sheet. The training meetings involve worship in song, prayer and testimony. There is motivation, teaching about ministry and about principles of being a successful lay pastor and TLC group leader.

Also at the meetings, the printed lesson is taught for the coming week. Most of the time the senior pastor writes these lessons. Often he ties them into a series that he is preaching on Sunday morning or an emphasis that he thinks the entire church needs at that time. When the senior pastor is out of town, one of the district pastors writes and teaches the lesson.

When the lay pastors enter a training meeting, one of the first things they see is their own district table. They place their reports in the box on the table and pick up new report sheets for the coming week. They pick up their lessons for the week. Also, there is an envelope that has within it assignments to new people, new members, prayer requests, new converts, TLC prospects and all the other work of ministry that needs to be done with people. The lay pastor takes the assignment, carries it out and then returns it, along with a report, to the box on the table the following week.

During each service at New Hope, everyone present is asked to fill out a communication card. On Monday morning, the information from these cards goes to the information center, where the necessary data is taken from the cards. By noon on Monday, the information goes to the district secretaries who, in consultation with their district pastors, prepare the assignments for the lay pastors for the week.[7]

New Hope School of Ministry

In addition to the training already mentioned, New Hope

*E*very Christian is to be a minister.
Therefore, we must train ministers
how to train ministers.

has its own school of ministry. Dale Galloway is president of the school, and Floyd Schwanz is dean. The mission of the New Hope School of Ministry is "to train men and women for leadership in a local church and to contribute directly toward the spiritual and numerical growth of the Church of Jesus Christ. The school is an extension of the need-meeting ministries of the New Hope Community Church in Portland, Oregon."[8] The school's three-fold purpose is:

- to better equip New Hope's lay pastors for their ministry;
- to train ministers who will become part of New Hope's staff in the years ahead;
- to become a training center for those who will reproduce these same need-meeting ministries in other places.[9]

The school of ministry is committed to a discipleship model of education, which they call the "Timothy plan." Second Timothy 2:2 states, "And the things that you have heard from me among many witnesses, commit these to faithful men who will be able to teach others also." They believe that "every Christian is to be a minister. Therefore, we must train ministers how to train ministers."[10]

Two Certificates Available
The first of the two programs available at the school, the one-year program, includes a prescribed course of biblical, doctrinal and ministerial studies, as well as a variety of practical experiences. This program consists of three nine-week terms and a total of 30 credit hours. Twenty-four of the credits are required and six are electives. Various seminars are also scheduled throughout the year and

credits are given toward the certificate of lay ministry. Students who successfully complete the one-year course with a cumulative grade point average of 2.0 are awarded the certificate. Attendance at the graduation service is required unless a written request is filed with the registrar's office.

The three-year program requires the student to choose a major area of ministry for preparation. The ministries offered for major areas of study at this time include: Bible, church growth and counseling. The requirements for one major must be satisfactorily completed in order to qualify for this pastoral ministry certificate. A major offers the student the opportunity to concentrate his or her study in a specific area of ministry, its biblical principles and practices. A pastoral advisor assists the student in choosing the classes most effective in training toward maximizing the individual's gifts and special interests. The student and advisor plan the required and elective courses of the major and indicate both the sequence and the credit hours required.

Minors in the three-year program are available, but not required for graduation. These other ministries for a special concentration of work include: children's ministry, evangelism/disciplemaking, marriage/family life, New Life Victorious, prayer/healing, singles' ministry, worship/praise, youth ministry.

The three-year program consists of nine nine-week terms and a total of 90 credit hours. Sixty of the credits are required and 30 are electives. Various seminars are also scheduled throughout the year and credits are given toward the certificate. Students who successfully complete the three-year course with a cumulative grade point average of 2.0 will be awarded the certificate of pastoral ministry. Attendance at the graduation service is required unless a written request is filed with the registrar's office.[11]

A booklet outlining registration and costs, entrance requirements, attendance requirements, withdrawals and refunds, course descriptions and any other information needed is available by contacting New Hope.

Supervising Lay Leaders

Once the lay pastors have been trained and the home cell groups established, New Hope has discovered seven things to watch for when supervising these lay pastor-led groups:

1. See if the leadership team is in place (leader, assistant leader, host/hostess);
2. See if the prospect list is up-to-date;
3. Check progress toward the TLC goal of one family added to membership every six months;
4. Names of target families;
5. Names of potential lay pastor trainees;
6. Use of the 21 Principles for Successful TLC groups.[12]

21 Principles for Successful Cell Groups

1. There are three elements in an effective home cell group, which must be put into use and kept in equal balance for the best results: sharing, conversational prayer and application of the Bible.
2. The more an individual participates in a home cell group, the more he or she receives from that meeting.
3. Begin and close with conversational prayer.

*T*he worst mistake a church can make is to divide the entire parish into parts and then assign a leader over each part, hoping to start a successful home cell program.

4. Respond lovingly and immediately to a need expressed.
5. The Bible must be the authority and the guidebook.
6. Encourage sharing within the group.
7. Don't allow doctrinal discussion that is divisive or argumentative.
8. Practice mutual edification.
9. Lead in love.
10. Follow-up on members between meetings is essential.
11. New members being brought into the group will keep it alive and growing.
12. Handle problem people away from the group on a one-to-one basis.
13. Don't allow people to confess anyone's faults but their own.
14. Don't allow anyone to do all the talking.
15. Be tuned up spiritually yourself.
16. Keep learning; don't have all the answers.
17. Hang loose and maintain a relaxed spirit in the group.
18. A good sense of humor is a valuable asset.
19. When you have a need in your own life, ask your home cell group for help.
20. When you have a problem or need help, quickly go to your pastor or leader and ask for it.
21. Remember, it's Christ who does the leading, not us.[13]

Prayer and Patience

The worst mistake a church can make is to divide the entire parish into parts and then assign a leader over each part, hoping to start a successful home cell program. The reason for this is that "people who have not been called and motivated by the Holy Spirit will never follow through on doing the work of ministry."[14] Start small. New Hope did. But dream big. Take the principles for lay pastor training outlined in this chapter and scale them down to a realistic size that will fit your church. If this seems too intimidating to try on your own, take advantage of New Hope's lay pastor super bowls, which are geared to help churches of all sizes get started in lay pastor ministry. Then pray. And be patient. Remember, it takes time to build leaders, and it takes leaders to build successful home cell groups.

NOTES

1. Dale E. Galloway, *20/20 VISION How to Create a Successful Church* (Portland, Oregon: Scott Publishing Co., 1986), 131.
2. Ibid., adapted from 133-134; New Hope Community Church Lay Pastor Training Manual, adapted from 16-17.
3. Dale E. Galloway, *20/20 VISION How to Create a Successful Church* (Portland, Oregon: Scott Publishing Co., 1986), adapted from 134.
4. Ibid., 135.
5. Ibid., 137.
6. Ibid., 138.
7. Ibid., adapted from 136-137.
8. New Hope School of Ministry handbook, 1.
9. Ibid., 1.
10. Ibid., 3.
11. Ibid., 5-6.
12. Dale E. Galloway, *20/20 VISION How to Create a Successful Church* (Portland, Oregon: Scott Publishing Co., 1986), 153.New Hope Community Church Lay Pastor Training Manual, adapted from 53.
13. Dale E. Galloway, *20/20 VISION How to Create a Successful Church* (Portland, Oregon: Scott Publishing Co., 1986), adapted from 113-122.
14. Ibid., 155.

CHAPTER TEN

THEN THEIR EYES WERE OPENED

*He took bread, blessed and broke it, and
gave it to them. Then their eyes were opened
and they knew Him.* Luke 24:30,31

The two travelers had walked with Jesus along the dusty
road to Emmaus, explaining to Him all that had happened
in the past days, but never recognizing Him as the risen
Savior. It wasn't until Jesus blessed and broke the bread
that "their eyes were opened and they knew Him" (Luke
24:31).

One of the keys to the phenomenal success in growth
and ministry at New Hope is their belief that blessing is
imparted through brokenness. People who have been broken and have found healing through the love of Jesus
Christ can better be used to minister blessing to others
experiencing similar brokenness. That is why it is so
important for those ministering to remember that it is
Jesus only who heals and restores. If that thought is
always kept at the forefront of their ministry, then those to

whom they are ministering will have their eyes opened and will see Jesus. That's when blessing begins, and dreams are born.

"It was as a direct result of the crushing pain and loss I suffered at the breakup of my first marriage that I am able to truly empathize with those experiencing pain and loss," says Pastor Galloway. "It was through my own brokenness that the dream that would eventually become New Hope Community Church was born."

Roy's Story

"Some time ago, I began praying in earnest that the Holy Spirit would reveal His will for me and bless me with the power, willingness and desire to carry out His will for my life. Slowly I began waking to the idea of my life being used by God for others. I began to realize, with some amazement, how the Lord could turn the degradation of my past into something good. I began to believe He could use me to help people with alcohol and drug problems.

"I began drinking when I was 13. We called it 'liquid courage.' By the time I turned 19, my record included a felony larceny and an undesirable discharge from the Army.

"The day I turned 21, I began working in my father's nightclub. I worked in the nightclub for the next 17 years. Amid the laughter and gaeity was much insanity and death. I remember vividly when a man shot one of the bartenders through the heart and then went out into the parking lot and blew his own head off. I'll never forget cleaning up his brains, or the shock on the young boy's face when he saw the bartender—his mother—dead behind the bar.

"As the years wore on, my drinking became all-consuming. How can I explain what my withdrawals were like? It was as if every cell in my body were vibrating madly in a high-pitched scream.

"The ravaging years of alcohol and drug addiction left me badly mangled. Then, praise God, healing began. It was a slow, arduous process. There were detox centers, hospitals, treatment centers, countless AA meetings, and, above all, New Hope Church and New Life Victorious.

"Christ's love, manifested to me through the nurturing of my New Hope family, combined with the blessing of being allowed to serve in the New Life Victorious ministry, have been the strongest forces in my recovery.

"I believe in New Hope and its need-meeting ministries. I pray to be a part of this body for the rest of my life. My goal is to be the resident alcohol and drug counselor for New Life Victorious. I believe that combining the wisdom and compassion I have gained as a result of my past experiences with the completion of a master's program in counseling psychology will enable me to be used by God for the blessing of others."

This is Roy Lucas's story. As he pursues his master's degree in counseling psychology, he serves in the lay pastor program at New Hope, leading a TLC group for recovering alcoholics at New Life Victorious. His is just one of many broken-to-bless stories at New Hope Community Church.

Sue's Story

Sue Honnell thought she knew about grief. Her father died when she was 27, and she missed him terribly. But even that loss did not prepare her for the intense devastation that so totally engulfed her when her husband died 14 years later.

"I cried buckets," she says. "I thought the pain would

never stop. When people tried to comfort me by assuring me I was young and would marry again, I cried even harder. I didn't want a new husband! I wanted my husband who had died to come back again. It took me a while to accept the fact that it just wasn't going to happen that way. Eventually I came to the point of realizing that I had to go on with my life. Even then, I resisted what I felt God was telling me—that there were new and exciting adventures ahead for me. Not only did I not want a new husband, I didn't want any new adventures, either!"

But as Sue began to move beyond her own pain to the place where she could recognize that same pain in others, she felt the call of God on her life to minister blessing out of her own brokenness. That was the beginning of Sue's involvement in New Hope's grief ministry, which consists of a six-week group session, as well as individual counseling.

"Some of these people who come to us for ministry have been so totally devastated, so crushed by their loss, that they hardly have the strength to go on," Sue explains. "Meeting others who are also groping their way through grief, as well as those who have successfully made it through, is like finally seeing a light at the end of their tunnel. How thankful I am that God was able to take my own grief and use it to help others!"

Rich's Story

Rich Kraljev is a man with clear-cut objectives, of which evangelism and discipleship have top priority. That hasn't always been the case.

Prior to 1972, Rich was probably one of the biggest, most formidable "flower children" in existence. He was 6'10" tall, weighed 325 pounds, had long hair and a full

Because of the miracles of restoration that God has performed in their lives, they are so in love with Jesus Christ that others can't help but sense that love flowing from them.

beard, and dressed in surplus military clothes. For 10 years he had spent his days and nights doing drugs and drinking himself into oblivion. But even in his drunken, drug-induced stupors, he knew something was missing in his life. He always felt as if he were searching—but for what? Then, on the night of October 14, 1972, he went to the home of his long-time friend and drug dealer to "score." And score he did, but certainly not in the way he had expected!

Rich hadn't seen his friend in a while. When he arrived at his house, the first thing the friend did was to tell Rich about his conversion to Christianity six weeks earlier. Whether out of curiousity or because of his own restlessness and searching, Rich listened. Before the night was over, his former drug dealer had led Rich to a decision to accept Christ as Savior. That same night, a speech impediment that had plagued Rich for 25 years disappeared.

"That made me very suspicious," Rich admits. "I got nervous because I figured God had plans for me. But I didn't really mind, because suddenly I knew I had a purpose in life. I wanted to go out and tell everyone about Jesus. And that's exactly what I did—whether they wanted to hear it or not!"

Immediately on fire for the Lord, Rich set out to convert the world. "I had a lot of enthusiam," Rich explained wryly, "but no tact! I'd grab people by the throat and explain to them about salvation. I don't know how much long-term success I had, but when I talked to them, they listened!"

It wasn't until he met Dale Galloway that he first realized his evangelism methods needed a little refinement. "It was in the very early days of New Hope. Dale Galloway looked beyond my gruff exterior and saw potential. He took me with him on one-to-one evangelism visits. I watched him gently, lovingly, lead people to Christ. Thanks to Dale, I became one of the first 10 lay pastors at New Hope."

Now a fulltime pastor and staff member, Rich no longer resembles a refugee flower child. Although still a tall, imposing figure, he dresses conservatively and pastors New Hope's large and active singles' ministry. Married and the father of three children, he also preaches on Sunday mornings or evenings in Dale's absence. But no matter how busy he gets with his family or work, he still sees evangelism and discipleship as his main goals in life. "However," he states emphatically, "thanks to Dale and the lay pastor training program at New Hope, I realize now that there are more effective ways to bring people to Christ than by sitting on their chest!"

The Key to Unlocking Successful Ministry

Roy Lucas, Sue Honnell and Rich Kraljev, as well as Dale Galloway and countless others at New Hope Community Church, have allowed God to take the brokenness of their lives and turn that brokenness into blessing. Because of the miracles of restoration that God has performed in their lives, they are so in love with Jesus Christ that others can't help but sense that love flowing from them. There is no more powerful force in the universe than divine, healing love. Realizing and appropriating that fact, as well as the the fact that God has chosen us as vessels through which that love is to flow to others is, without a doubt, the key to unlocking successful ministry for each and every individual in each and every church throughout the entire world. As we begin to move into that type of ministry, our testimony will also be, "Then their eyes were opened and they knew Him . . . . "